TIME

Queen Elizabeth II

1926 - 2022

Contents

The World's Longest-Serving Monarch

BY LARRY SUTTON AND STEVE DOUGHERTY

Her extraordinary reign, which began in 1952, spanned over a dozen British prime ministers and U.S. presidents. She inherited the throne of a country almost broken by the legacy of war, and remained upon it through a time of epochal change both for the U.K. and the world.

Yet she remained a stoic, almost timeless figure in the public's eye, carrying out her royal duties both large and small even when her private life was in turmoil, and despite the inconvenience of advancing age.

When Elizabeth took the throne, the U.K. was the seat of an Empire that straddled the globe. Today, Britain is a smaller player on the world's stage, but the Queen remained the sovereign leader of 15 nations—including Australia, Canada, and New Zealand—and head of a Commonwealth of more than 50 nations. She traveled the globe as an ambassador for British achievements, acts of charity, and values. She was also devoted to upholding the "special relationship" between the U.K. and the U.S., engaging with every president from Harry Truman to Joe Biden over a period of more than 70 years.

The world changed while Elizabeth was Queen in profound ways, but many saw her as a steadfast rock of patriotic duty. As her grandson Prince William wrote in the preface to a 2015 biography: "I think I speak for my generation when I say that the example and continuity provided by the Queen is not only very rare among leaders but a great source of pride and reassurance... I am privileged to have the Queen as a model for a life of service to the public."

BORN AN HEIRESS

Elizabeth Alexandra Mary Windsor was born by cesarean section at 2:40 a.m. on Apr. 21, 1926. She was an heir to the throne, but third in the line of succession. Her father, Prince Albert—"Bertie" to friends and family—was the second son of the reigning monarch, King George V. His older brother, Edward, known as David to close friends and family and as Edward of Wales to the public, was first in line to the throne. But he was also single, childless, and already rumored to have little interest in inheriting his father's crown and the duties that went with it.

The early life of Princess Elizabeth was chronicled with zeal both by the British press and in the former colonies. "The water was from the River Jordan," TIME reported of the elaborate christening pageantry staged in the private chapel at Buckingham Palace. Sir Winston Churchill first met Elizabeth at Balmoral Castle in 1928, when she was just 2, and proclaimed that he saw in her "an air of authority and reflectiveness astonishing in an infant."

Future Queen *Elizabeth (center) on the balcony of Buckingham Palace on the day her father was named King George VI.*

"I am privileged to have the Queen as a model for a life of service to the public."

—PRINCE WILLIAM

No one in all the realm was more enamored with the young Elizabeth than its monarch, who nicknamed her Lilibet and gave her the place of honor on his lap when they rode through the streets of London in his royal stretch Daimler. "No one else except the Queen rides out so often with the king," TIME reported. Left, not ungladly, out of the spotlight was Lilibet's father—the ever-reticent in public, self-deprecating Bertie, who once told reporters, "My chief claim to fame seems to be that I am the father of Princess Elizabeth."

Her reign as only child ended at age 4, in 1930, with the birth of her sister, Margaret Rose, at Glamis Castle in Scotland, their mother's ancestral home. The girls romped together on the palace grounds and royal country estates, played with their terrier puppies and corgis—Elizabeth's lifelong favorite. They also stabled, cared for, and learned to train a succession of royal pet ponies, and shared the same nannies and governesses.

In January 1936, upon the death of Lilibet's grandfather George V, her uncle Edward became King Edward VIII. Almost immediately, his eldest niece and all the royal family became prime players in a 20th-century succession drama that, though bloodless, proved riveting to a worldwide audience. Edward's tumultuous 10-month reign as king ended on Dec. 10, 1936, when he scandalized the world by abdicating the throne to marry the twice-divorced American socialite Wallis Warfield Simpson. "I always told those idiots not to put me in a golden frame," he said. Young Lilibet was only 10 when she learned she would one day become queen after her father's death.

PRINCESS IN WARTIME

Elizabeth was barely a teenager when, on Sept. 3, 1939, Britain declared war on Nazi Germany. The war's threat had already thundered throughout Europe, and soon the kingdom Elizabeth would one day rule, along with much of the rest of the world, was engulfed in war. Less than a year later, Hitler entered Paris and promised to make Britain his next conquest. Soon the Blitz—day and night Luftwaffe bombing raids that rained fire and terror

Leading by Example *Elizabeth (right) and her sister Margaret prepare for a children's address during WWII.*

over London, Liverpool, and other cities throughout England—was at full roar.

And so the Princess spent her teens knitting socks for British soldiers, collecting tinfoil, and rolling bandages for the war effort. She would send portions of her five-shilling weekly allowance to emergency child welfare funds, wear secondhand clothes, adhere to the war rations diet dictated for all Britons, and live frugally despite being a teenage princess and heir to the British throne.

Even as bombs fell on Buckingham Palace—it was hit nine times, including once in September 1940, but the King and Queen managed to escape unharmed—the royal couple refused entreaties to abandon London and evacuate Princess Elizabeth and Princess Margaret to Canada. "The children won't go without me," said the Queen. "I won't leave without the King. And the King will never leave."

The King's decision to remain in England for the duration of the war, enduring its deprivations along with his subjects, endeared him to the beleaguered nation. But it also made the likelihood that Elizabeth might suddenly be called to the throne in the event of her father's death seem palpable.

The future monarch began her public life with her first live BBC radio broadcast in October 1940. Displaying poise and pluck, she addressed the tens of thousands of children who were evacuated from their homes and separated from their families at the height of the Blitz. "My sister, Margaret Rose, and I feel so much for you as we know from experience what it means to be away from those we love most of all," she said in a clear voice that offered a hint of the calm and compassion that many would come to admire.

When she reached military age at 18 in 1944, Elizabeth joined the Auxiliary Territorial Service, one of the wartime women's units. She spent three weeks at the Mechanical Transport Training Center, where she trained as a mechanic and truck driver. The labor left her covered in grease and grime and not a little well-earned pride. "Everything I learnt was new to me—all the oddities of the insides of a car," she told a friend. "I've never worked so hard in my life!"

And she never partied so hard as she did a fortnight after her 19th birthday when, on May 8, 1945—Victory in Europe Day—she joined the ecstatic and rowdy street celebrations that swept London following Germany's surrender. After standing in uniform on the balcony at Buckingham Palace to greet cheering crowds alongside the King, Queen, and Prime Minister Winston Churchill, she, her sister, a group of friends, and a few guardians linked arms and ran among the crowds that surged through the city. For two nights in a row she "walked simply miles," she wrote in her journal, "ate, partied, bed 3am!" These were, she would say 40 years later, among "the most memorable nights of my life."

ROYAL WEDDING

It wasn't long after the war that the young princess turned her mind to thoughts of marriage. Years before, Elizabeth had visited a naval college at Dartmouth where she had been greeted by a towering 18-year-old cadet.

Prince Philip of Greece and Denmark was born on the Greek island of Corfu on June 10, 1921, nephew of King Constantine of Greece and distant relation to Britain's Queen Victoria. As his family drifted apart, he was sent off to England at age 9 to live with his grandmother, the widow of the great British naval commander and German prince Louis Alexander Mountbatten. He was schooled in England, Germany, and Scotland, and became a fine young athlete—as Elizabeth would note to her governess, Crawfie, on that trip to Dartmouth: "How good he is, Crawfie. How high can he jump!"

Elizabeth corresponded with Philip throughout the war, and after its end the Prince was placed on shore duty at a naval base on England's south coast. He often made the 100-mile trek to London in his small black MG, frequently stopping at Buckingham Palace to have dinner with Elizabeth and her younger sister, Margaret. Their friendship grew into a romance. Elizabeth was delighted. Her father George? Not so much—at first. "His loud, boisterous laugh and his blunt, seagoing manners…irritated the gentle king," TIME reported in 1957. Despite that chill, Elizabeth and Philip decided to marry after a short stay with her family at Balmoral Castle in the summer of 1946. The King's lack of enthusiasm for Elizabeth's beau—an attitude sparked, in part, by his concern over how the people of Britain would take to a foreign-born prince marrying the heiress to the throne—frustrated the Princess. "There was many a tense moment for George as Elizabeth moped about in tearful martyrdom while her mother and grandmother, the doughty old Queen Mary, fought her battle for her. At last, George decided that the young couple (she was 20, he 25) should wait six months to make sure of each other," noted TIME.

There were obstacles to overcome, but none insurmountable. Philip became a British citizen, and public opinion polls showed that a majority of the nation's populace favored his marrying the Princess. The official announcement did not come until July 9, 1947, followed by the couple's introduction at a Buckingham Palace garden party. The wedding took place that November, on the 20th. Philip had converted from Greek Orthodoxy to Anglicanism, avoiding one social problem before the ceremony, and Elizabeth's father made the former member of the Greek and Danish royal families a British royal duke, the Duke of Edinburgh, to be called His Royal Highness, or simply Prince Philip.

As Elizabeth made her way to Westminster Abbey in the royal coach on her wedding day, thousands cheered from the neighboring sidewalks of London. Celebrations erupted throughout the globe, from Paris to Panama, from Shanghai to Manhattan—where thousands got out of bed at 6 a.m. to listen to the ceremony broadcast on the radio. Dignitaries—five kings, six queens, Prime Minister Clement Attlee, Winston Churchill—were in attendance. All of Britain celebrated, many seeing the wedding as a beacon of hope in the post-World War II recovery period.

THE CORONATION

On Feb. 5, 1952, Princess Elizabeth went to bed in a tree hut nestled in Kenya's Aberdare National Park and awoke the next day as the Queen of England. She was unaware of her new position, for news of the death of her father, King George VI, had not yet reached that outpost of the British Empire. That afternoon, at a lodge, Philip received a phone call informing him of

the King's death. The Prince took his bride down to a nearby river's edge and relayed the news. Shaken but in full command of herself, Elizabeth returned to the lodge on Philip's arm and began making arrangements for the long trip home.

Elizabeth arrived at London's airport the following morning. Churchill was there to greet her, along with a small group of privy councilors—advisers to the monarchy. That night she rested; the next day she signed the oath of accession before the Privy Council, and an hour later her accession was formally proclaimed. In the months that followed, there was no hurry to arrange her formal coronation—she was already, technically, the Queen. So Elizabeth and the Palace allowed the focus to stay on King George and his 16 enormously popular years on the throne, and let the nation's sadness ebb.

The official ceremony finally took place on June 2, 1953, a day chosen in hopes of sunny spring weather. This being London, however, the nation settled for a traditional gray morning. At 11 a.m., a joyous fanfare of trumpets announced the arrival of Her Majesty. "Vivat Regina Elizabetha! Vivat! Vivat! Vivat!" shouted the Queen's Westminster Scholars as she walked up the aisle, her long crimson train borne by six maids of honor. The Archbishop of Canterbury proceeded to ask Elizabeth if she would govern her people according to their laws and customs, execute law and justice in mercy, and maintain the laws of God. She knelt, kissed the Holy Bible before her, and swore to do so, "so help me God." Finally, he held aloft the Imperial State Crown for all to see, then placed it on Elizabeth's head. Cheers of "God Save the Queen" filled the Abbey as trumpets blared; outside, and across the British Empire, bells pealed and cannons roared.

THE TRAVELING QUEEN

As well as the constitutional duties Elizabeth fulfilled as Britain's head of state and the head of the Church of England, she spent long sections of the following decades traveling the world as her nation's goodwill ambassador. The November after her coronation, she embarked on a 45,000-mile tour of the British Commonwealth, presiding over state balls, garden parties, luncheons, banquets, and other occasions. Among her stops: Libya, Australia, Fiji, New Zealand, Jamaica, Uganda, and the Pacific island of Tonga, where she enjoyed the company of Queen Salote Tupou, who had traveled to London months before to witness Elizabeth's coronation. She did not return to London until May 15, 1954, almost six months after she departed.

In the fall of 1957, Elizabeth and Philip spent six days in New York City, Washington, D.C., and parts of

Making Appearances *Meeting the king of Ashanti and African chiefs with Philip in Kumasi, Ghana, in 1961.*

Virginia, where they celebrated the 350th anniversary of the founding of Jamestown, the first British colony in America. In Washington, they were guests of President Dwight D. Eisenhower—a friend since his days in London as Supreme Allied Commander during World War II—for four nights at the White House. At the president's state dinner, Elizabeth praised Washington as "so often a focus for the aspirations of the free world." Later, Vice President Richard Nixon hosted a luncheon at the Capitol, and Elizabeth sought to see how the average American enjoyed life, attending a football game at the University of Maryland and stopping in a Giant supermarket after the game.

Clearly, the travel bug had bitten. In 1961, Elizabeth visited India, and at the Ramlila Ground near Old Delhi, a quarter-million people came to see her speak. In the city of Jaipur, the Maharajah offered her a ride on a ceremonial elephant. Though the trip was a success for Elizabeth, it also put the Indian government on edge—they viewed such a display of colonial pageantry as undermining the country's fledgling independence. Philip also drew negative publicity when official photos emerged of a tiger he'd killed on a hunt with the Maharajah An Indian government spokesperson called the act "astonishing," while the British tabloid *The Daily Mirror* condemned the royals for not recognizing "the modern enlightened view on the killing of animals for pleasure."

In Ghana that same year, Prime Minister Kwame Nkrumah told the Queen, "The wind of change blowing through Africa has become a hurricane." (Ghana declared independence from the British Empire in 1957, though the legacy of colonialism still loomed over the country.) Tanzania would declare independence later that year, joined by Kenya in 1962, and a series of other African nations throughout the 1960s.

In 1965, Elizabeth embarked on an 11-day tour of West Germany, the first state visit by a reigning British monarch since Edward VII paid his last call on Kaiser Wilhelm II in 1909. The trip came a full two decades after the end of World War II, amid fears of lingering resentment between the U.K. and Germany. But those fears were misplaced. The Queen and German Chancellor Ludwig Erhard said all hostility between their countries had been healed in the 20 years since the war. It ended in triumph, with crowds cheering and chanting "Elizabet, Eliz-a-bet!" as she placed a wreath on a Beethoven monument near Bonn City Hall.

FAMILY TROUBLE

All that traveling would put a strain on her family. That 5½-month world tour following her coronation took place when Charles was 5 and Anne only 3—but the children were left behind. They did chat with their traveling mother by radiotelephone. But this would go on to be characteristic of Elizabeth, who always tended to make work her priority.

Years later, in 1994, Prince Charles would allow his authorized biographer to disclose that the Prince felt "emotionally estranged" from his parents, who were "unable or unwilling" to offer the affection he craved as a young man. Close friends found the Duke's behavior "inexplicably harsh" and called his manner toward Charles "very bullying." His mother, the Queen, seemed "detached." Elizabeth and Philip were reported to be hurt by this disclosure. Publicly, only Philip would comment, "We did our best." But Princess Anne, the couple's daughter and Charles's younger sister, exercised less restraint—and in the process defended Elizabeth from rumors that she was remote and uncaring as a mother. "I simply don't believe that there is any evidence whatsoever to suggest that she wasn't caring," she said in 2002. "It just beggars belief. We as children may have not been too demanding, in the sense that we understood what the limitations were in time and the responsibilities placed on her as monarch in the things she had to do and the travels she had to make. But I don't believe that any of us, for a second, thought she didn't care for us in exactly the same way as any other mother did."

Yet even Anne might have acknowledged a warmth that was sometimes wanting on her part later in life—when a little more compassion, a little more kindness, might have been called for.

The early 1990s would bring all kinds of personal problems to the fore—most notably in 1992, which the Queen famously described in a speech as an "annus horribilis" (horrible year). This was the year when her second son, Andrew, separated from his wife, Sarah; when daughter Anne divorced her husband, Mark Phillips; when her son Charles and his wife, Diana, increasingly became a tabloid issue; and when public concern grew about the cost of the monarchy and who would pay to repair Windsor castle, which caught on fire that year.

The damage was significant. The Nov. 20 fire—on the Queen's 45th wedding anniversary—gutted the northeast corner of the castle, parts of which were more than 900 years old. It took 250 firefighters 15 hours to bring it under control. The state apartments, used for high-level official entertaining, did not have a sprinkler system, and in the end more than 100 rooms, covering an area of 1.7 acres, were damaged.

When British citizens learned that they were about to foot the bill for repairs to Windsor Castle—to the tune of up to $78 million—they grumbled. Elizabeth rectified the issue by volunteering to pay income and capital gains tax from her private investments. It hurt, but not too much: Her net worth remained at about $500 million.

Together Time *The royal family (Edward, Elizabeth, Philip, Anne, Andrew, and Charles) on the grounds of Frogmore Cottage, Windsor, in 1968.*

But these were simply matters of state. It was matters of the heart that caused greater grief for Elizabeth—particularly the travails of Charles and Di.

Their courtship and 1981 marriage captivated the nation, if not the world. No less an authority than the Archbishop of Canterbury proclaimed, "Here is the stuff of which fairy tales are made: the prince and princess on their wedding day." But infidelity would intrude on both sides, and the ability to maintain even the pretense of marriage for the sake of appearances became impossible. On Aug. 24, 1992, the transcript of a phone conversation between Diana and a close friend was published in The Sun tabloid, with Diana describing life with Charles as "real torture," and saying she had caught the Queen Mother watching her "with a strange look in her eyes." Diana and her young sons, William and Harry, continued to reside at Kensington Palace, while Charles's relationship with Camilla Parker Bowles was parsed by the tabloid press. The Prince and Princess of Wales officially separated on Dec. 9.

Diana's decision to grant an interview to the BBC on Nov. 20, 1995, in which she confessed that she had been unfaithful to Charles, had upset the royal family and Queen Elizabeth in particular. (Of course, Charles had admitted his own infidelity on a TV documentary the previous year, as Diana noted in the interview, referring to Camilla Parker Bowles, "There were three of us in this marriage, so it was a bit crowded.") Within a month, the Queen wrote to both Charles and Diana, urging them to agree to an early divorce. Buckingham Palace released a statement saying Charles favored the divorce, but there was no official word from Diana. In February 1996—more than a year before Diana, her romantic partner Dodi Fayed, and driver Henri Paul died in a car crash while being pursued by the paparazzi—she finally released her own statement saying she was ready to divorce too. Elizabeth's reaction? "The Queen was most interested to hear that the Princess of Wales had agreed to the divorce," was all her press office would say at first. Later, it would announce that the Queen wished the divorce discussions "be conducted privately and amicably."

It took time for Elizabeth—a woman married seven decades to the same man—to adjust to modern mores. A longtime sticking point was Charles's future bride, Camilla; the press noted that Elizabeth was not enamored of her son's consort. The turning point occurred in 2002, when, by bringing Camilla to events celebrating Elizabeth's 50 years on the throne, Charles provided strong evidence that he was gaining ground in his campaign to bring Camilla officially into the family fold.

Charles and Camilla got engaged around Christmas 2004, and before long the Queen issued a statement saying, "The Duke of Edinburgh and I are very happy that the Prince of Wales and Mrs. Parker Bowles are

to marry." She and Prince Philip did not attend their wedding at Windsor Guildhall on April 9, 2005, but they did attend a blessing of the couple at St. George's Chapel in Windsor Castle and held a reception for them at the castle.

A more festive wedding—and one more in keeping with Elizabeth's sense of royal tradition—took place on Apr. 29, 2011, when Elizabeth's grandson William married Kate Middleton in a lavish ceremony at Westminster Abbey. And she remained her regal self at Prince Harry and Meghan Markle's more modern wedding at Windsor Castle in 2018, which included a fiery sermon delivered by Bishop Michael Curry of Chicago, the first African American head of the Episcopal Church in the U.S.

The Queen would face further familial scandals, however. In a televised interview with Oprah Winfrey in March 2021, Harry and Megan alleged that racism had tarnished their relationship with the Windsors. While the press hounded Megan like they did Harry's late mother, "no one from my family ever said anything," Harry said.

The family was once again thrust into the spotlight when allegations surfaced about Andrew's relationship with the late sex offender, Jeffrey Epstein. Andrew stepped back from royal duties in late 2019, and in 2021 was served with a lawsuit by Virginia Giuffre, one of Epstein's victims, who accused Andrew of sexually abusing her when she was 17. According to *The Daily Telegraph*, the Queen contributed millions of pounds to her son's legal defense, and agreed to contribute £2 million ($2.7 million) to a victim support charity as part of the eventual settlement.

As the Queen neared the end of her life, she doted more on her grandchildren and great-grandchildren. "In a small room with close members of the family, then she is just a normal grandmother. Very relaxed," Harry said before he and Meghan stepped back as working royals in early 2020. "She obviously takes a huge interest in what we all do, that's her children as well as her grandchildren. She wants to know which charities we're supporting, how life is going in our jobs and such. So you know, she has a vested interest in what we do."

ROYAL DUTY

Even after she entered her ninth decade, Elizabeth continued with her royal duties, despite her age and a rapidly changing world.

Each day, the Queen would read a selection of letters that she received, as well as review official papers and documents sent her way from government ministers and her representatives in foreign countries. Until she was forced to slow down by mobility issues and bouts of ill health, she would have 10- to 20-minute audiences

‘

"We could not be more proud of her. She has served this country with unerring grace, dignity, and decency."

—FORMER PRIME MINISTER, DAVID CAMERON

with ambassadors, commissioners, and other officials, and there would be her weekly visit from the British prime minister (Liz Truss, who was sworn in a few days before the Queen's death, was her 15th PM).

Despite growing republican movements within the Commonwealth realms, the Queen herself remained a hugely popular figure in both the U.K. and beyond. And she remained a force for good, offering messages of inspiration and optimism in even the most trying times. In one of her last annual Christmas Day messages, she urged her subjects in Britain and across the Commonwealth to draw inspiration from "ordinary people doing extraordinary things."

The Queen has been a constant figure in most of the British public's living memory—in February 2022 she became the first British monarch to reach 70 years on the throne. Although mobility issues prevented her from attending the majority of Buckingham Palace's Platinum Jubilee celebrations in June of the same year, community celebrations were widespread across the U.K. Some 16,000 official street parties were organized and almost 17 million people—about one in four Brits— took part in events. The Together Coalition, which aims to bridge divides, said the celebrations were the largest community event in British history.

The Queen also looked extraordinary yet ordinary at Prince Philip's funeral held shortly after he died on April 9, 2021, after 73 years of marriage. The image of the monarch solemnly sitting alone in a pew at Windsor Castle due to coronavirus restrictions became instantly iconic, and further burnished her image as a stoic leader through good times and bad.

The Queen did not lead an ordinary life, but she filled it with extraordinary acts of duty both public and private—whether carrying out the requirements of the state from the trappings of the throne, or giving quiet words of encouragement to a well-wisher in a crowd. She "has been a rock of stability in an era in which our country has changed so much," said Britain's former Prime Minister David Cameron. "And we could not be more proud of her. She has served this country with unerring grace, dignity, and decency."

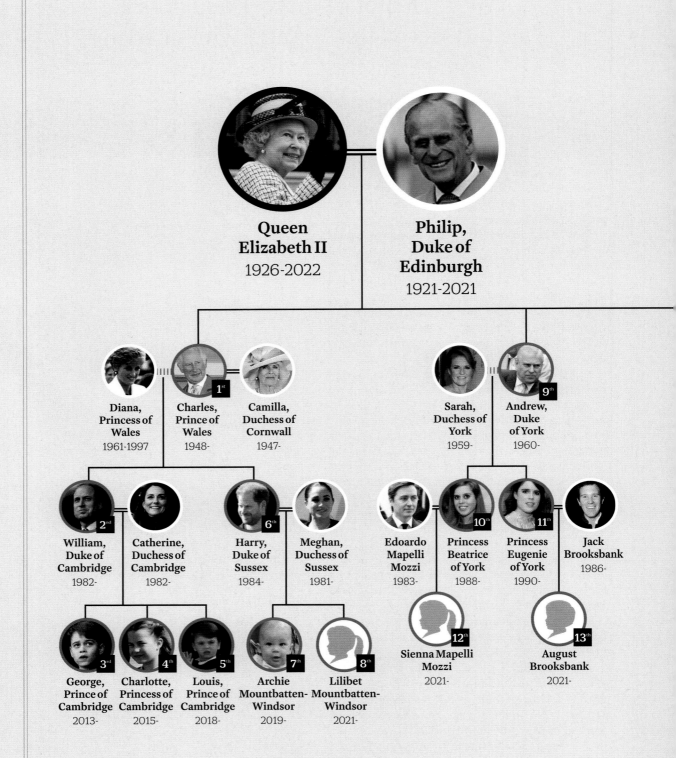

Queen Elizabeth II
1926-2022

Philip, Duke of Edinburgh
1921-2021

Diana, Princess of Wales
1961-1997

1st
Charles, Prince of Wales
1948-

Camilla, Duchess of Cornwall
1947-

Sarah, Duchess of York
1959-

9th
Andrew, Duke of York
1960-

2nd
William, Duke of Cambridge
1982-

Catherine, Duchess of Cambridge
1982-

6th
Harry, Duke of Sussex
1984-

Meghan, Duchess of Sussex
1981-

Edoardo Mapelli Mozzi
1983-

10th
Princess Beatrice of York
1988-

11th
Princess Eugenie of York
1990-

Jack Brooksbank
1986-

3rd
George, Prince of Cambridge
2013-

4th
Charlotte, Princess of Cambridge
2015-

5th
Louis, Prince of Cambridge
2018-

7th
Archie Mountbatten-Windsor
2019-

8th
Lilibet Mountbatten-Windsor
2021-

12th
Sienna Mapelli Mozzi
2021-

13th
August Brooksbank
2021-

Who Is Next in Line?

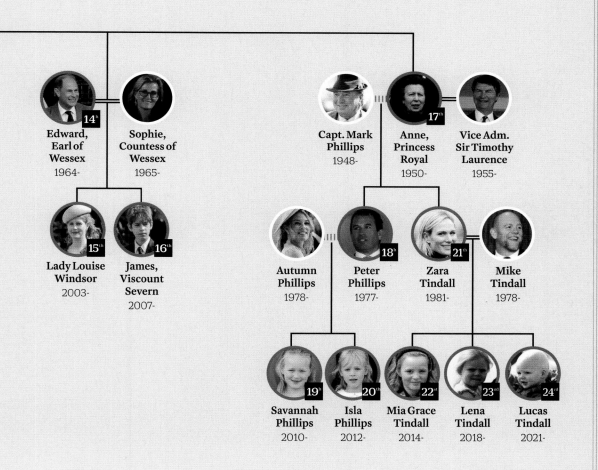

Edward, Earl of Wessex 14ᵗʰ
1964-

Sophie, Countess of Wessex
1965-

Capt. Mark Phillips
1948-

Anne, Princess Royal 17ᵗʰ
1950-

Vice Adm. Sir Timothy Laurence
1955-

Lady Louise Windsor 15ᵗʰ
2003-

James, Viscount Severn 16ᵗʰ
2007-

Autumn Phillips
1978-

Peter Phillips 18ᵗʰ
1977-

Zara Tindall 21ˢᵗ
1981-

Mike Tindall
1978-

Savannah Phillips 19ᵗʰ
2010-

Isla Phillips 20ᵗʰ
2012-

Mia Grace Tindall 22ⁿᵈ
2014-

Lena Tindall 23ʳᵈ
2018-

Lucas Tindall 24ᵗʰ
2021-

Her Family Legacy

Get to know the immediate family the Queen
left to follow in her footsteps.

Family Photo *Prince Charles,
Princess Anne, the Queen, Prince
Andrew, and Prince Philip during a
visit to Balmoral Castle in 1960.*

THE CHILDREN

Charles, Prince of Wales
BORN NOVEMBER 14, 1948

 Charles is the eldest son of Queen Elizabeth and heir to the throne. He has committed to a lifetime of service—he was a member of the Royal Air Force and the Royal Navy, and has worked with or overseen over 400 charities. He is particularly interested in the environmentalist movement and preserving historic architectural principles. He was an avid sportsman and polo player in his youth.

Anne, Princess Royal
BORN AUGUST 15, 1950

 Anne had an equestrian career and competed in the 1976 Montreal Olympic Games. She devotes a lot of her time to children's causes, including Save the Children UK, where she served as president since 1970. She also travels extensively on official visits and engagements to support over 300 charities.

Prince Andrew, Duke of York
BORN FEBRUARY 19, 1960

 Andrew was a career naval officer who served in the Falklands War. Over his lifetime, Andrew focused on public work causes, particularly in business and economics. He was officially stripped of his royal and military titles in Jan. 2022 following allegations of sexual abuse of a minor."

Prince Edward, Earl of Wessex
BORN MARCH 10, 1964

 Edward is the youngest child of the Queen and has dedicated his life to public service for young people. When Prince Philip died, he took over the Duke of Edinburgh's Award, which is an international program to help children develop life and work skills, and he oversees The Earl and Countess of Wessex Trust, which supports youth-oriented charities. He also supports sports, the arts, and the armed forces—he holds eight military titles.

THE ROYAL SPOUSES

Vice Admiral Sir Timothy Laurence
BORN MARCH 1, 1955

 Married Anne, Princess Royal December 12, 1992 Timothy, a career naval officer, was awarded the rank of Vice Admiral in 2007 and retired in 2010. Since then, he has spent his time on property and regeneration charity work, tennis, golf, sailing, field sports, and battlefield tours.

Sophie, Countess of Wessex
BORN JANUARY 20, 1965

 Married Edward, Earl of Wessex June 19, 1999 As a full-time member of the royal family, Sophie served the queen by visiting various schools, universities, military bases, and charities. She is a patron of over 400 charities and is invested in supporting people with disabilities, preventing avoidable blindness in developing countries, and contributing to agriculture and sustainable fashion causes.

Camilla, Duchess of Cornwall
BORN JULY 17, 1947

 Married Charles, Prince of Wales April 5, 2005 Camilla contributes to over 90 charities, including organizations dedicated to health, literacy, poverty, the elderly, animals, the arts, and women's rights, and those that support victims of rape, sexual abuse and domestic violence.

THE GRANDCHILDREN

Peter Mark Andrew Phillips

BORN NOV. 15, 1977

Son of Anne, Princess Royal and Mark Phillips (divorced 1992) Married Autumn Kelly (divorced 2021)

Zara Anne Elizabeth Tindall

BORN MAY 15, 1981

Daughter of Anne, Princess Royal and Mark Phillips (divorced 1992) Married Mike Tindall July 30, 2011

Prince William, Duke of Cambridge

BORN JUNE 21, 1982

Son of Charles, Prince of Wales and Diana, Princess of Wales (divorced 1996) Married Catherine Middleton (Duchess of Cambridge) April 29, 2011

Prince Harry, Duke of Sussex

BORN SEPT. 15, 1984

Son of Charles, Prince of Wales and Diana, Princess of Wales (divorced 1996) Married Meghan Markle (Duchess of Sussex) May 19, 2018

Princess Beatrice of York

BORN AUGUST 8, 1988

Daughter of Prince Andrew, Duke of York and Sarah, Duchess of York (divorced 1996) Married Edoardo Mapelli Mozzi July 17, 2020

Princess Eugenie of York

BORN MAR. 23, 1990

Daughter of Prince Andrew, Duke of York and Sarah, Duchess of York (divorced 1996) Married Jack Brooksbank October 12, 2018

Lady Louise Windsor

BORN NOV. 8, 2003

Daughter of Prince Edward, Earl of Wessex and Sophie, Countess of Wessex

James, Viscount Severn

BORN DEC. 17, 2007

Son of Prince Edward, Earl of Wessex and Sophie, Countess of Wessex

Proud Grandmother *A few of the grandkids appear on the balcony of Buckingham Palace for the Trooping the Colour festivities in 1998.*

A Growing Family *Princess Charlotte and Prince George hold hands with their father as their mother cradles the infant Prince Louis before his christening service in 2018.*

THE GREAT-GRANDCHILDREN

Savannah Anne Kathleen Phillips

BORN DEC. 29, 2010

Daughter of Peter Phillips and Autumn Kelly (divorced 2021)

Isla Elizabeth Phillips

BORN MAR. 29, 2012

Daughter of Peter Phillips and Autumn Kelly (divorced 2021)

Prince George of Cambridge

BORN JULY 22, 2013

Son of Prince William, Duke of Cambridge and Catherine, Duchess of Cambridge

Mia Grace Tindall

BORN JAN. 17, 2014

Daughter of Zara and Mike Tindall

Princess Charlotte of Cambridge

BORN MAY 2, 2015

Daughter of Prince William, Duke of Cambridge and Catherine, Duchess of Cambridge

Prince Louis of Cambridge

BORN APRIL 23, 2018

Son of Prince William, Duke of Cambridge and Catherine, Duchess of Cambridge

Lena Elizabeth Tindall

BORN JUNE 18, 2018

Daughter of Zara and Mike Tindall

Archie Harrison Mountbatten-Windsor

BORN MAY 6, 2019

Son of Prince Harry, Duke of Sussex and Megan, Duchess of Sussex

August Philip Hawke Brooksbank

BORN FEB. 9, 2021

Son of Princess Eugenie of York and Jack Brooksbank

Lucas Philip Tindall

BORN MAR. 21, 2021

Daughter of Zara and Mike Tindall

Lilibet Diana Mountbatten-Windsor

BORN JUNE 4, 2021

Daughter of Prince Harry, Duke of Sussex and Megan, Duchess of Sussex

Sienna Elizabeth Mapelli Mozzi

BORN SEPT. 18, 2021

Daughter of Princess Beatrice of York and Edoardo Mapelli Mozzi

Royal Names, Explained

Here's the story behind the use of last names in the royal family.

BY MEGAN MCCLUSKEY

A Worldwide Affair
Prince William and the newly named Duchess of Cambridge greet the crowds following their nuptials.

Watched by Millions *Prince Harry and the new Duchess of Sussex leaving St. George's Chapel after their wedding ceremony in 2018.*

JUST AS THE QUEEN BESTOWED THE royal title Catherine, Duchess of Cambridge to Catherine Middleton at her wedding to Prince William in 2011, the Queen gave Meghan Markle the title of Duchess of Sussex when she married Prince Harry in 2018. A lot has changed since then, and the flurry surrounding the royal family ignited renewed interest in the naming conventions of its members.

When Harry and Meghan announced the name of their baby boy in 2019, they revealed that his full name, Archie Harrison Mountbatten-Windsor, includes the royal surname. And in 2021, they named their daughter Lilibet Diana Mountbatten-Windsor, which was an homage to the Queen's nickname, Lilibet, and a tribute to Harry's late mother, Diana. But where did Mountbatten-Windsor come from? Turns out, it's a story steeped in love and war.

WHAT IS THE ROYAL FAMILY'S LAST NAME?

The royal family's naming practice may seem complicated, but the reason behind it is relatively simple: The royals are typically so well known that they don't need a last name to be recognized. "Members of the Royal Family can be known both by the name of the Royal house, and by a surname, which are not always the same," the official royal website reads. "And often they do not use a surname at all."

This means that Prince Harry's full name could technically be Henry Charles Albert David Mountbatten-Windsor and that Meghan could have become Rachel Meghan Mountbatten-Windsor following their wedding. However, considering last names are typically only used by members of the royal family without a title, you don't need to worry about tacking the hyphenated surname onto Harry and Meghan's names.

Members of the royal family can also use a last name from their family's official title. For example, Prince Harry and Prince William were known at school and in the military as Harry Wales and William Wales, a surname that derived from their father's official title, the Prince of Wales. Prince George, meanwhile, has taken the surname Cambridge at school, from his father's title as Duke of Cambridge.

Basically, when in doubt about how to refer to a member of the royal family, first names and titles are the safe way to go.

> ' The royals are typically so well known that they don't need a last name to be recognized.

WHAT WAS QUEEN ELIZABETH'S LAST NAME?

Princess Elizabeth Alexandra Mary Windsor was born to the Duke and Duchess of York—later King George VI and Queen Elizabeth, the Queen Mother—on April 21, 1926. She became next in line to the crown when her father, King George VI, ascended the throne following the abdication of her uncle Edward VIII, in 1936. Princess Elizabeth was born into the royal House of Windsor, making her last name—if she needed it—Windsor.

Queen Elizabeth was born with the last name Windsor, but that wouldn't have been the case before 1917. That year, her grandfather King George V (shown at right with his wife, Queen Mary) decided to switch his house name from Saxe-Coburg-Gotha to Windsor in order to head off anti-German sentiments during WWI. This also designated Windsor as the royal family's official surname going forward.

Before 1917, British royals went only by their first names and the name of the house or dynasty they belonged to, such as Tudor or Hanover—i.e., Queen Victoria of the House of Hanover.

WHERE DID THE NAME MOUNTBATTEN-WINDSOR COME FROM?

Following Elizabeth's marriage to Lieutenant Philip Mountbatten (later Prince Philip, Duke of Edinburgh)—in 1947 and her ascension to the throne in 1952, Queen Elizabeth II made a slight adjustment to her grandfather's naming decree by adding a hyphenated "Mountbatten" to the last name of her descendants to reflect the surname of her husband.

Today, the last name of the British royal family remains Windsor. However, royals who are descended from Queen Elizabeth II through the male line use the hyphenated surname Mountbatten-Windsor when needed. This last name reflects both the surname of the royal family and that of the Queen's late husband and love of her life, Prince Philip.

Family Memories Through the Years

Despite her relentless engagement schedule and the pressures of being a monarch, Queen Elizabeth always valued family time. Here are some of the special moments.

MARCH 1932

Kids Will Be Kids *An almost 6-year-old Princess Elizabeth riding her new tricycle in the park with her nanny and Princess Margaret (in the carriage).*

MAY 1937

All the Finery *Eleven-year-old Elizabeth (third from right) with her parents and sister posing in the robes they wore for her father's coronation as King George VI.*

AUGUST 1951

In the Highlands *Queen Elizabeth, Princess Margaret, Prince Philip, King George VI, and Princess Elizabeth with her children, Prince Charles (left) and Princess Anne, at Balmoral Castle in Scotland less than a year before King George VI died.*

MAY 1942

A Fine Family *Princess Margaret, Queen Elizabeth, Princess Elizabeth (then 16), and King George VI at Buckingham Palace in May 1942.*

SEPTEMBER 1952

A New Queen *Anne, Philip, Charles, and Elizabeth at Balmoral Castle seven months after she took the throne.*

SEPTEMBER 1960

A Picnic Together *Baby Prince Andrew perches on his father's lap (center) during a picnic on the grounds of Balmoral Castle. Also pictured are Anne, Elizabeth, and Charles.*

DECEMBER 1971

Memory Lane *Elizabeth looking at a photo album with her sons Andrew (left) and Edward. Footage of this scene was used in the Queen's Christmas Broadcast in 1971.*

AUGUST 1972

Silver Wedding Anniversary *The family gathers for a group portrait at Buckingham Palace. Standing, left to right: Charles, Anne, Andrew, and Philip. Seated: Edward and Elizabeth.*

JANUARY 1979

The Men in Her Life
*Elizabeth posing rather
formally with Philip
and their sons (Andrew,
Charles, and Edward) at
Balmoral Castle.*

JULY 1985

Rare PDA *Charles
charmingly kisses his
mother's hand after the
Cartier Polo Match.*

JUNE 1999

Sweet Moment *Prince Harry gives his granny a kiss after having tea at Guards Polo Club in Windsor Great Park.*

JUNE 2003

Three Generations *Elizabeth poses with Prince Charles, Prince William, and Prince Philip at Clarence House, London.*

NOVEMBER 2007

Celebrating 50 Years
Charles (front row) joins his parents, along with his siblings (back row), Andrew, Anne, and Edward, to mark the royal couple's diamond wedding anniversary.

JUNE 2015

Happy Birthday *The family gathers on the Buckingham Palace balcony waiting to view the flyby at the Trooping of Colour, the Queen's annual birthday parade. Front: Princess Anne; Camilla, Duchess of Cornwall; Prince Charles; Prince William holding Prince George; Queen Elizabeth; James, Viscount Severn; and Prince Philip. Back: Catherine, Duchess of Cambridge; Prince Harry; Prince Andrew; and Princess Eugenie of York.*

DECEMBER 2016

Royal Appearance *The Queen poses with her family before the annual evening reception for members of the Diplomatic Corps at Buckingham Palace. Camilla, Duchess of Cornwall; Prince Charles; Prince Philip; Prince William; and Catherine, Duchess of Cambridge.*

JUNE 2017

With the Grandkids
The Queen smiles at Princess Charlotte and Prince George on the Buckingham Palace balcony at the annual Trooping of Colour. Also shown: Vice Admiral Sir Timothy Laurence; Princess Beatrice of York; Prince Philip; Princess Anne; Catherine, Duchess of York; and Prince William.

Princess to Queen

An unlikely set of circumstances put Elizabeth on the throne.

BY ELIANA DOCKTERMAN

ELIZABETH DIDN'T EX-
pect to be the Queen. Born
on April 21, 1926, to King
George V's second son, Prince
Albert, the Duke of York, she was
third in line to the throne. Albert's
older brother Edward, Prince of
Wales, had not yet married, but
the family was confident he would
settle down and have children soon.
So the Duke and Duchess of York
planned a life largely out of the
spotlight for Elizabeth and their
second daughter, Margaret.

Precious Times *King George VI
and Queen Elizabeth with Princesses
Elizabeth and Margaret on the
grounds of Windsor Castle in 1936.*

A DEATH AND AN ABDICATION

When Elizabeth was still small, her uncle Edward began spending a great deal of time with American divorcée Wallis Simpson, to the consternation of the palace. Kings were not allowed to marry divorced women. Rumors swirled about their relationship, though Edward maintained to his family that Simpson was just a good friend. The King and Queen became outraged with Edward when he invited Simpson to the King's Silver Jubilee Ball in 1935.

The possible affair was a mainstay in American gossip columns—the British press was silent on the matter—but the situation graduated to a national crisis in Britain on Jan. 20, 1936, when King George V died. The loss stung Elizabeth. She had adored him and was one of the only people in the country who seemed to be unafraid of him. The archbishop of Canterbury was rather taken aback when he once caught Elizabeth leading the King by the beard as if he were a horse. Meanwhile, the adults of the family worried about Edward's intentions with Simpson now that he had been named King Edward VIII.

Their fears were confirmed when Wallis filed for divorce from her second husband. On Nov. 16, 1936, Edward summoned Prime Minister Stanley Baldwin to Buckingham Palace to declare his intention to marry Wallis and make her queen. Baldwin informed the King that the British people would not accept this on religious grounds: Edward was the titular head of the Church of England and therefore bound by its restrictive divorce laws.

But Edward followed his heart, and on Dec. 10 he announced his abdication of the throne. He had ruled for just 325 days. A footman informed Elizabeth and Margaret of the news. Margaret asked her 10-year-old sister, "Does that mean you will have to be the next queen?"

"Yes, someday," Elizabeth replied.

"Poor you," said Margaret.

A RELUCTANT KING

Margaret likely picked up such sentiments from her father. Albert was a reluctant king. He wrote that he "broke down and sobbed like a child" when discussing his brother's abdication with his mother. Albert had not been groomed to be a king. He'd never seen a state paper in his life and dreaded public speaking because of a stammer he hadn't been able to overcome. But duty-bound, Albert took the name of King George VI to send a message of continuity in a tumultuous time. He soon moved his family into Buckingham Palace.

Her Father Accedes *King George VI greets the crowd on the Buckingham Palace balcony on his coronation day, May 12, 1937.*

Elizabeth had been on the cover of TIME at the tender age of 3, but now the Princesses became a national obsession in the U.K. King George VI had always resented being the less favored brother, so he insisted that no one show preference for Elizabeth over Margaret. As a result, the sisters dressed identically, and their outfits would instantly sell out in department stores. Despite his efforts to treat them equally, the King soon slotted his daughters into their respective roles. Elizabeth was the serious one: She meticulously lined up her shoes in her room every night before bed and would leap up from mid-sleep if she thought one was out of order. Margaret was the more precocious and sociable one.

On the Farm *Eighteen-year-old Elizabeth poses with a horse at Sadringham House in Norfolk.*

HAPPINESS OVER EDUCATION

Despite the fact that Elizabeth was now heir apparent, the King and Queen did not prioritize Elizabeth's and Margaret's education. Some biographers have speculated that the King did not want his daughters to be able to outsmart him. It's certainly true that the Queen believed only women who would eventually hold jobs should go to school. Apparently, being a queen barely qualified as a career, since the Princesses received just one and a half hours of schooling per day.

Marion Crawford, called Crawfie by the family, tutored the Princesses at home. Their classes focused more on handwriting than on science and statecraft. The two girls did learn about the history of the royal family. And at 13, Elizabeth began to attend private lessons with the vice-provost of Eton College, Henry Marten. They studied the ins and outs of the British constitution for six years.

Elizabeth and Margaret had a sheltered childhood. They attended birthday parties thrown by the daughters of neighbors, but any excursion into London attracted so much attention that the girls never had a hope of feeling ordinary. Crawfie enlisted the daughters of palace workers and noblemen to create a troop of Girl Guides (a British version of Girl Scouts) for the Princesses. They built campfires to earn badges. Elizabeth also developed a fondness for horses and dogs. Her father gifted her the first in a long line of corgis, Dookie, in 1933. She has owned more than 30 in her lifetime.

WORLD WAR II

Any sense of normalcy disappeared for Britain when World War II began. In 1940, the two Princesses were ferried away to Windsor Castle, about 20 miles from London, for safety and stayed there for five years until the Allies defeated Germany. Their parents stayed in Buckingham Palace, undeterred by the bombings. The Queen notoriously would not be rushed to the bomb shelter during raids. Once, Buckingham Palace received a direct hit, nearly killing the royal couple. The Queen wrote to her mother later that she had been trying to remove an eyelash from the King's eye when they heard the sound of a plane above. "It all happened so quickly that we had only time to look foolishly at each other when the scream hurtled past us and exploded with a tremendous crash in the quadrangle," she wrote. Later she claimed she was glad the palace had been bombed so that she could face the citizens in the East End who had borne the brunt of the German attacks.

Windsor was safe from such chaos. Though she hosted friends and officers there, Elizabeth seemed to live in a suspended childhood. She missed debutante season, and at the urging of her mother, she continued to wear childish clothing through her 18th birthday. Her one moment of independence came in early 1945 when her father permitted her to train for three weeks at the Mechanical Transport Training Centre as part of the war effort.

Princess Bride *Elizabeth waves to the crowd from the balcony at Buckingham Palace shortly after she wed Prince Philip.*

A ROYAL COURTSHIP

In May 1945, Elizabeth and Margaret returned to London. England had survived the war, and so had Philip, Elizabeth's third cousin. The Princess had set her heart on the tall, blond sailor five years her senior, and not even international upheaval could change her mind.

Louis "Dickie" Mountbatten, Philip's uncle, arranged for Philip to have lunch with the royal family at the Royal Naval College in Dartmouth when Elizabeth was 13. When Philip went on to serve in the British Royal Navy, the two kept in touch. When Elizabeth was 17, Philip visited the royal family for Christmas. He watched as Elizabeth performed in a pantomime of Aladdin. Soon after, Elizabeth's grandmother wrote to a friend that the two had "been in love for the past eighteen months. In fact longer, I think."

THE WEDDING

Elizabeth was steadfast. Philip proposed to her in the summer of 1946, and the 20-year-old immediately accepted without consulting her parents. Her father consented on the condition that they wait until her 21st birthday to announce the engagement. The wedding was set for Nov. 20, 1947. The morning of the ceremony Philip quit smoking "suddenly and apparently without difficulty," according to his valet, as a romantic gesture. Elizabeth detested the habit because of the toll it had taken on her father's health. The King gave Elizabeth away, even though he knew it meant the breaking up of the tight-knit royal family. "When I handed your hand to the Archbishop, I felt I had lost something very precious," he later wrote to Elizabeth.

Several guests were conspicuously missing from the wedding in Westminster Abbey. Philip's sisters were not invited because of their German husbands and the family's Nazi affiliations. Elizabeth's uncle Edward was also barred from the wedding for political reasons: The palace believed that if the former King were to attend, the British people might view him as a threat to his brother's reign.

Like Queen Victoria before her, Elizabeth insisted that during the ceremony she promise to "obey" her husband, though her family and some in the government had urged against it. Over the course of their marriage, Elizabeth would try to make such conciliatory gestures to her husband.

The Road to

January 20, 1936
Elizabeth's grandfather, George V, dies. His son, Edward VIII, accedes to the throne.

1933
Elizabeth receives her first corgi as a gift from her father.

August 21, 1930
Princess Margaret is born.

December 1943
Philip visits the royal family for Christmas.

December 10, 1936
Edward VIII abdicates. His younger brother, George VI, becomes King.

1926

April 21, 1926
Princess Elizabeth is born.

1930

1931
Prince Edward meets Wallis Simpson.

1934
Elizabeth meets Philip Mountbatten at a royal wedding.

November 16, 1936
Edward VIII announces his intention to marry Simpson, an American divorcée, resulting in scandal.

1940

September 1, 1939
World War II begins. The Princesses are sent to Windsor for safety while their parents remain at Buckingham.

April 21, 1944
Elizabeth turns 18.

H.R.H. PRINCESS MARGARET ROSE   H.R.H. PRINCESS ELIZABETH

the Throne

Early 1945
Elizabeth serves in the Auxiliary
Territorial Service in the war effort.

September 2, 1945
World War II ends.

November 20, 1947
Elizabeth and Philip marry
at Westminster Abbey.

1949
Philip is stationed
in Malta, so the new
family moves to the
Mediterranean.

August 15, 1950
Princess Anne
is born.

February 6, 1952
George VI dies
and Elizabeth
becomes Queen.

1950

May 1945
Elizabeth
returns to
London.

Summer 1946
Philip proposes
to Elizabeth.

November 14, 1948
Prince Charles
is born.

September 1951
Elizabeth's father,
George VI, becomes
seriously ill with
cancer.

June 2, 1953
Queen Elizabeth II
is crowned at
Westminster Abbey.

SHORT-LIVED ADVENTURES

About a year later, Elizabeth gave birth to the couple's first child, Charles. Philip took to renovating their new home, and in 1949 they moved into their first house together. That same year, Philip was appointed second-in-command of a destroyer off the island of Malta, and they moved to the Mediterranean. The couple had another child, Anne. They lived happily, Philip embarking on his naval career and Elizabeth experiencing life outside the spotlight for the first and only time in her life.

King George VI had long had health problems, and in 1951 he took a turn for the worse. In September, surgeons removed the King's left lung after finding a malignancy. The family kept the news from the press, but Elizabeth's private secretary, Martin Charteris, took to carrying a draft accession declaration in case the King died when Elizabeth was out of the country. In January 1952, Elizabeth and Philip set off for Kenya, the first stop on a royal tour meant to be taken by the King. When they arrived, the couple spent an evening in a hotel perched in a tree, and Elizabeth, who nurtured a lifelong love of photography, filmed elephants meandering below.

A NEW QUEEN

On the morning of Feb. 6, King George VI died at age 56. The news spread across England, and Prime Minister Winston Churchill reportedly bemoaned the fact that Elizabeth, at 25, was "only a child." Yet no one was able to reach Elizabeth and Philip, still gazing at the wildlife from the treetop hotel in Kenya. It took approximately four hours to get hold of the couple. Philip broke the news to Elizabeth, and Charteris asked what she was going to call herself. (Monarchs often adopt new names, as Elizabeth's father, Albert, had done.) Elizabeth answered, "My own name, Elizabeth, of course. What else?"

Perhaps naively, Elizabeth and Philip had not expected her to inherit the crown so soon. Philip had planned for a long naval career before he became a full-time husband, and he struggled to play the role of consort. He protested their move into Buckingham Palace and bristled under Elizabeth's newfound authority. Elizabeth's mother and sister were also left with little purpose now that the King was gone. Their lives "must seem very blank," Elizabeth wrote, while hers had a newfound meaning.

Still, some were cheered by the news. Margaret Thatcher, who would later become the first fe-

Starting a Family *Elizabeth and Prince Philip with Prince Charles and Princess Anne in the summer of 1951.*

male prime minister, wrote in a newspaper column at the time, "If, as many earnestly pray, the ascension of Elizabeth II can help to remove the last shreds of prejudice against women aspiring to the highest places, then a new era for women will indeed be at hand." And when Elizabeth arrived in London, Churchill was among the first to endorse her: "Famous have been the reigns of our queens. Some of the greatest periods in our history have unfolded under their scepter."

Philip's uncle Dickie Mountbatten greeted the news clumsily. "The House of Mountbatten now reigns," he announced. Elizabeth's grandmother heard rumors of the declaration and teamed up with Churchill to persuade Elizabeth to keep the name House of Windsor, lest she risk backlash from the people against her foreign-born husband. Elizabeth agreed, and Philip balked. "I am the only man in the country not allowed to give his name to his children," he complained to friends. "I'm nothing but a bloody amoeba."

"If, as many earnestly pray, the ascension of Elizabeth II can help to remove the last shreds of prejudice against women aspiring to the highest places, then a new era for women will indeed be at hand."

—MARGARET THATCHER

A Leader Emerges *Princess Elizabeth smiles at the crowds while visiting the West Midlands in 1951— one year before she became Queen.*

A Sovereign Is Born *Newly crowned Queen Elizabeth II and Philip greet onlookers on her coronation day.*

THE CORONATION

To assuage Philip, Elizabeth gave him the job of heading up the committee to organize her coronation. He pushed to modernize the event for the young female monarch by bringing cameras into Westminster Abbey. Queen Elizabeth and Churchill initially nixed the idea but changed their minds when they found the public was in favor of televising the event. It was the first major international event to be broadcast on TV.

Elizabeth's uncle Edward was again left off the invitation list. He reportedly said of the snub, "What a smug, stinking lot my relations are." But the former king, who had never had his own coronation, tuned in to the ceremony on June 2, 1953, along with 20 million other people around the world.

Three million onlookers gathered in the streets to cheer as the Elizabeth made her way to Westminster Abbey in a 24-foot-long gold stagecoach. She wore a dress adorned with the symbols of Great Britain and the Commonwealths, including a rose, a thistle, a shamrock, a maple leaf, and a fern. In the abbey, the most sacred part of the ceremony was hidden from the cameras: Elizabeth was anointed with holy oil under a canopy. Holding a scepter and balancing a five-pound solid-gold crown on her head, the Queen took her throne.

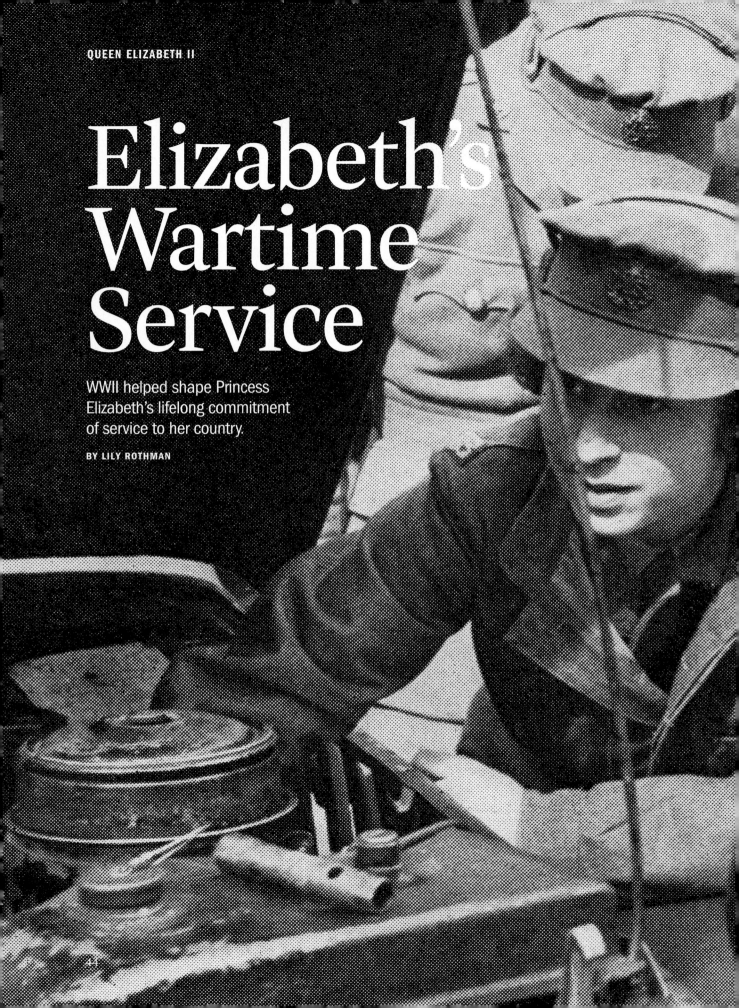

Elizabeth's Wartime Service

WWII helped shape Princess
Elizabeth's lifelong commitment
of service to her country.

BY LILY ROTHMAN

A YOUNG FEMALE AUTO MECHANIC IN military uniform in England in 1945 would not have been a rare sight, nor would a photograph of one such woman giving a demonstration to a visiting dignitary. This particular photo, however, is unusual because of what her job was when she wasn't serving in the Auxiliary Territorial Service (ATS), a women's army auxiliary branch.

The visiting dignitary is Queen Elizabeth—now perhaps better known as the Queen Mother—and the young ATS subaltern is her daughter, the future Queen Elizabeth II.

Under the Hood *In this famous photograph, Princess Elizabeth shows her mother a thing or two about engines while serving in the ATS in 1945.*

WOMEN'S WARTIME CONTRIBUTIONS

In 2018, the photo was displayed in "Women in WWII: On the Home Fronts and the Battlefronts" at the International Museum of World War II in Natick, Massachusetts (the museum closed in 2019). The show took a wide view of the many roles played by women from every nation involved in the conflict, and this photo was one of the documents in the exhibition that best underlined the active role women sought during the war.

"To me, it's a really interesting example of women's roles in the war. Women wanted to be part of what was going on. They were a part of what was going on. It fits in with the statement made by Elizabeth's mother, Queen Elizabeth, that when Buckingham Palace was bombed she felt she could look the East Enders in the eye," says Kenneth Rendell, the former museum's director.

In 1939, as TIME reported in a cover story on British women at war, the impact of the war on the nation's women was widespread and immediate. Career girls lost their work as unnecessary businesses shut down, housewives coped with austerity measures, mothers sent their children to safety in the countryside, and thousands signed up to fill auxiliary military roles as well as essential civil jobs, from driving buses to milking cows, that were left vacant as men went into combat. At Buckingham Palace, the older Queen Elizabeth officially became the commandant-in-chief of the Women's Royal Naval Service, Women's Auxiliary Air Force and Women's Auxiliary Territorial Service. Their uniforms, the magazine declared, were "the first warlike garments to be worn by an English Queen since the days of Boadicea." And her daughters Princess Elizabeth and Princess Margaret were, like so many young Britons, sent away from London for protection from the Blitz.

And, when Princess Elizabeth turned 18 in 1944, LIFE magazine would report, she advocated for herself to serve the way other young Brits would have to.

THE KING HESITATES, THEN COMMISSIONS HIS DAUGHTER

"[The] King ruled after long deliberations with his councilors that her training as a princess outweighed the nation's increasing manpower problems and that 'Betts' should not join any of the women's auxiliaries, nor work in a factory," the magazine related. "But Betts had other ideas. It was not surprising that not long afterward the Palace made a straight-face announcement that the King 'had been pleased to grant an honorary commission as second subaltern in the ATS to Her Royal Highness the Princess Elizabeth.'"

The Princess' desire to serve was in keeping with the overall mood in her homeland, Rendell says: "People have said to me that the lucky ones were the pilots, because they were doing something."

Princess Elizabeth, heiress presumptive to the throne, was commissioned as an honorary second subaltern in the ATS—basically the equivalent of a second lieutenant—and began training in March of 1945. Per royal decree from her father the King, she was given no special rank or privilege. (She did later earn a promotion to junior commander.) At the time, the Associated Press reported that she was the first woman in the royal family to be "a full-time active member in the women's service."

PRINCESS ELIZABETH'S WORK

Though not a combat role, serving in the ATS was not without its risks. The service saw its first death in 1942, when a woman serving at an anti-aircraft station was killed by a bomb. Nor was it something those with privilege sought to avoid; Winston Churchill's daughter Mary also served in the ATS.

Once she joined up, the Princess passed a military driving test, learned to read maps, and worked repairing engines. (She did sleep at Windsor Castle, though, rather than in the camp with her fellow ATS members.)

According to the official War Office caption printed on the back of the photo, the King and Queen and Princess Margaret visited an ATS training center in the south of the country and watched Princess Elizabeth learn about auto maintenance. In the photo, the Princess explains her work with the engine to the Queen. An Associated Press report on the April 9 visit dubbed the future sovereign "Princess Auto Mechanic."

In addition to serving the country, she took her time with the ATS as a valuable lesson in what life was like for non-royals—including just what went into the scene shown in the photograph. "I never knew there was quite so much advance preparation [for a royal visit]," LIFE quoted the Princess as saying. "I'll know another time."

Valuable Skills
Princess Elizabeth changes a tire at an ATS training center in 1945.

'

Once she joined up, the Princess passed a military driving test, learned to read maps, and worked repairing engines.

The Love of Her Life

We reveal the story behind the man who knew Elizabeth best.

BY SALLY BEDELL SMITH

Young Prince Philip
(clockwise from left) Eyeing up flowers at the age of 1; playing cricket while at Gordonstoun in 1939; acting in a production of Macbeth (seated) in 1935; and wearing traditional Greek dress at age 9.

A TOUGH START FOR A PRINCE

Standing 6 feet, the 18-year-old naval cadet cut a striking figure: piercing blue eyes, tousled white-blond hair, and perfectly chiseled features. No wonder Prince Philip of Greece and Denmark instantly captured the heart of Princess Elizabeth, the diminutive heiress presumptive to the British throne. When they encountered one another on a midsummer day in 1939, she was only 13, but behind Philip's handsome facade she detected the verve, intelligence, sharp wit, and quiet fortitude that would put her phlegmatic British aristocratic swains to shame. "She never looked at anyone else," said Elizabeth's first cousin and confidant Margaret Rhodes.

Like the Princess's, Philip's great-great-grandparents were Queen Victoria and Prince Albert, while his father's family was descended from a Danish prince recruited for the Greek throne in the mid-19th century. But Philip had neither fortune nor vast landed estates. He was, in fact, a royal vagabond relying on the generosity of relatives who gave him shelter, paid his school fees, and kept him fed and clothed.

He was born on the island of Corfu on June 10, 1921. Eighteen months later, his parents, Princess Alice of Battenberg and Prince Andrew of Greece and Denmark, whisked him out of the country with his four older sisters after Philip's uncle King Constantine I was deposed in a coup. Andrew's wealthy older brother gave the penniless family a small house outside Paris, where Philip attended the American school in Saint-Cloud, a suburb of Paris.

At age 8, Philip was packed off to Cheam, a boarding school in England, and his mother's family, the Milford Havens and Mountbattens, took charge of his upbringing. The following year Alice had a mental breakdown and was committed to a sanatorium. Andrew moved to Monte Carlo with a mistress, where he subsisted on a small annuity. Philip was typically stoic: "I just had to get on with it. You do. One does." His uncle Louis "Dickie" Mountbatten, Alice's ambitious younger brother, would become Philip's surrogate father.

Athletic and assertive, Philip thrived in the "spartan and disciplined" atmosphere at Cheam. In 1933 he transferred to Salem, a boarding school in Germany run by a progressive Jewish educator named Kurt Hahn. The rise of the Nazis forced Hahn to flee to Scotland, where he founded the Gordonstoun School on the North Sea coast in 1934. Philip enrolled soon afterward. The school's harsh physical regimen and emphasis on community service deeply imprinted the rootless young prince, who rose to become the school's head boy. Hahn said Philip had a tendency toward "recklessness" as well as "impatience and intolerance"—traits Philip would strive to check as an adult.

FINDING LOVE WITH A PRINCESS

Soon after Philip began his training at the Royal Naval College of Dartmouth, his wily Uncle Dickie, an officer in the British navy, arranged an afternoon with King George VI, Queen Elizabeth and their two daughters, Princess Elizabeth and Princess Margaret. The spark was struck, and Philip and Elizabeth corresponded while he served during World War II with the Royal Navy in the Pacific and the Mediterranean.

On leave in London, the nomadic Greek Prince visited Windsor Castle, and a romance with Elizabeth blossomed. He had "a capacity for love which was waiting to be unlocked," said his first cousin Patricia Mountbatten. "Elizabeth unlocked it."

When his father died in 1944 of cardiac arrest at age 62, he left his remaining worldly goods to his son: some clothing, an ivory shaving brush, cuff links and a signet ring. After her release from the psychiatric clinic, Philip's mother settled in Athens, withdrew from the world and established a Greek Orthodox sisterhood of nuns. Essentially orphaned, Philip welcomed the generous hospitality offered him by Elizabeth's parents, thanking Queen Elizabeth for "the simple enjoyment of family pleasures and amusements."

In the summer of 1946, the 25-year-old Philip proposed to 20-year-old Elizabeth, who accepted instantly. Before their marriage, on Nov. 20, 1947, he renounced his Greek titles, adopted Mountbatten as his surname, and became a British citizen. He also converted from the Greek Orthodox faith to the Church of England. The King named his son-in-law the Duke of Edinburgh, invested him with the ancient Order of the Garter, and declared that he should be called His Royal Highness. On the morning of his wedding, Philip stubbed out his last cigarette as a favor to his bride.

FLEETING PRIVATE FAMILY TIME

On Nov. 14, 1948, Elizabeth and Philip's first child and heir to the throne, Charles Philip Arthur George, was born in a hospital suite at Buckingham Palace. They had scarcely a year together as a family in London before the Royal Navy posted Philip to Malta. Back in his element, he rose rapidly up the ranks from first lieutenant to lieutenant commander in charge of the frigate *HMS Magpie*.

But at age 30 his military career abruptly ended in July 1951 when Elizabeth was summoned to London to take on duties from her father, who was suffering from lung cancer. "There was no choice. It just happened," Philip later said. "I tried to make the best of it."

During a five-week trip across Canada and to Washington, D.C., that autumn, Philip showed his irreverent streak, joking with bystanders to put them at ease—all designed to "puncture the balloon," in the words of his friend Sir David Attenborough. Thus began a lifetime of "gaffes" gleefully recounted—and often misquoted—by the press.

With King George VI in decline, Philip and Elizabeth stepped in to undertake his planned six-month world tour, starting with a brief idyll in Kenya. There, after a night in a game preserve, Philip learned that the King had died in his sleep on Feb. 6, 1952, and his wife was now Queen. He gently broke the news and comforted her on the long flight home.

‘He had "a capacity for love which was waiting to be unlocked. Elizabeth unlocked it."

—PRINCE PHILIP'S COUSIN PATRICIA MOUNTBATTEN

A Joyous Event *(opposite page) Philip and Elizabeth share a loving gaze on their wedding day in 1947.*

New Parents *The young couple proudly show off their first child, Prince Charles.*

On Tour *Sharing a moment aboard the destroyer* Crusader *while on their Commonwealth Tour in 1951.*

HUSBAND OF THE QUEEN

The new Queen's starchy courtiers took a dim view of Philip's unorthodox background and worried he would try to impose modern ideas on the traditional court. All the qualities admired by Elizabeth—his breezy charm, inquisitive mind and forthright manner—disquieted the "gray men" who advised her. He was "constantly being squashed, snubbed, ticked off, rapped over the knuckles," said his friend Lord John Brabourne. In private, Philip was impatient and restless, occasionally lashing out to call his wife "a bloody fool." He mordantly referred to himself as the "refugee husband."

The most wounding rebuff was Elizabeth's decision to keep the family name of Windsor for their children rather than his adopted surname of Mountbatten. The issue would simmer until the Queen approved a compromise in 1960 calling for those in the direct line of succession to be named Windsor while descendants without the "royal highness" designation would carry a Mountbatten-Windsor surname.

Philip had no place in the substance of his wife's official life—her state papers and dealings with the government. But he was a crucial modernizing force behind the scenes. He advised the Queen on the operation of the royal household, applying what one of her advisers called his "defense staff rigor" to analyze proposals and offer suggestions. At Philip's urging, she began hosting informal Buckingham Palace lunches for "meritocrats" drawn from a range of fields to keep her connected to the outside world.

A LEADER EMERGES

He nudged his wife to accept televised coverage of her coronation in 1953 and four years later persuaded her to switch from radio to television for her annual Christmas message, which he helped write. He coached her on public speaking and on how to use a teleprompter. He stood behind the camera, and when she concluded, she flashed him a luminous smile.

An enthusiast for technology since his days in the navy, Philip was the first member of the royal family to embrace computers. "I can claim to have petted the first microchip on the head," he once said. In the 1980s he began sending emails and later became an avid user of Google, eagerly sharing his findings with his wife. He encouraged the Queen's communications team to set up a website in 1997 as a way to promote more direct contact with the public.

Crucially, the Queen designated him head of the family—"the natural state of things," she said—responsible for decisions about the education of their children, including Princes Andrew and Edward, born in the 1960s. He was a stern taskmaster, especially in his efforts to toughen the sensitive Charles. Rather than speaking about personal matters face-to-face, the paterfamilias and his eldest son relied mainly on written communication, leading to decades of misunderstanding.

When the troubled marriage of Charles and Diana ruptured in 1992, Philip wrote her a series of letters counseling compromise, to no avail. It was Philip who persuaded Prince William and Prince Harry to join their mother's funeral cortege in September 1997. "If I walk, will you walk with me?" he asked. Seven years later, William described his grandfather as "someone who will tell me something that maybe I don't want to hear … I'm glad he tells me."

GIVER TO MANY

Philip was often away from home—sometimes for months at a time—acting as the Queen's global ambassador. His trips allowed him to recapture the freedom of his former life, but he also used them to expand his portfolio of enterprises and philanthropies. He became an active patron of more than 800 charities, their focus ranging from sports, youth opportunity, and fitness to science and conservation. Since its founding in 1956, his most famous initiative, the Duke of Edinburgh's Award, has helped millions of young people across the globe build self-reliance and confidence by meeting physical and mental challenges.

While his formal education had been spotty, Philip became a determined self-educator, compiling a library with thousands of volumes. He wrote his own speeches, and by 1989 he was the author of 10 books that included essays on religion, philosophy, and science. He made a televised plea for preserving rainforests decades before Prince Charles took up the same cause. But when the heir to the throne made a forceful denunciation of genetically modified crops during a BBC Radio lecture in 2000, his father publicly disagreed with him. "You've got to stick your neck out," Philip said, or "you'd end up living like a cabbage."

He began to shed some of his patronages, but he remained absorbed by causes that had gripped him since his youth. In 2016 he carried out 219 public engagements, significantly more than the 188 undertaken by Prince William, 60 years his junior. After being briefly sidelined with a heavy cold over Christmas that year, Philip was back out on the circuit in 2017. Inspecting a new system to diminish pollution on London buses, he quizzed the experts on the finer points of battery storage technology, and on a visit to the new National Cyber Security Centre, he advised officials to hire more people who "do not pre-date the internet."

THE PROMISE KEPT

During his honeymoon with Elizabeth in 1947, Philip had written a letter vowing "to weld the two of us into a new combined existence that will not only be able to withstand the shocks directed at us, but will have a positive existence for the good." Over the next seven decades, as the longest-serving royal consort to the longest-serving British monarch, Philip became what his wife called her "strength and stay" and fulfilled his pledge until his death in April 2021.

Sally Bedell Smith is a historian and the author of the bestselling biography Elizabeth the Queen: The Life of a Modern Monarch.

A Reign of Hope and Stability

Elizabeth led her realm with noble
service, strength, and endurance.

BY A.N. WILSON

THE BRITISH NATIONAL ANTHEM—"GOD Save the Queen"—is that rare thing: a prayer that was answered. "Long to reign over us!" the British sang when the young woman succeeded her father, George VI, during that cold February in 1952. They were still singing it 70 years later.

Half a Century *A radiant Elizabeth leaves St. Paul's Cathedral on the day of the service to mark her Golden Jubilee in 2002.*

"I declare before you all that my whole life, whether it be long or short, shall be devoted to your service."

—QUEEN ELIZABETH II

The Queen (*above*) *A newly crowned Elizabeth waves from the balcony after her coronation in 1953.*

Making the Rounds (*right*) *Greeting children during a Silver Jubilee walkabout in London in 1977.*

Cheers to 25 Years (*facing page*) *Elizabeth attending a performance at Covent Garden during her Silver Jubilee celebrations in 1977.*

Long to reign over us during Britain's grabbing me-me-me years of the Thatcher era, when Elizabeth alone seemed able to effectively tell the government that it had gotten South Africa wrong, that the Commonwealth had gotten it right, and that Nelson Mandela would one day be a free man. Long to reign over the United Kingdom while Ireland was in a state of war, and as, little by little, peace with a kind of honor came to the north. Long to reign over us as Britain came to realize it was a European nation (albeit a rather uneasy member of the E.U.). Long to reign over us when Britain voted to come out of the E.U., whose citizens were multinational, multiracial, and multi-faith. Long to reign over a U.K. that sat agog in 1953, watching Elizabeth II being crowned, the first time the ceremony had ever been televised. The longest-reigning British monarch. The longest-serving living head of state in the history of the world.

SHE DID NOT CHANGE

It was fully 45 years ago that Philip Larkin, the esteemed British poet, spoke for so many admirers when he penned this short quatrain:

> In times when nothing stood
> But worsened or grew strange,
> There was one constant good
> She did not change.

No other period of British history saw so much change. And this, surely, is what made the Queen such a very remarkable figure. She saw it all, lived through it all. And the old woman who still went to Parliament and bravely greeted foreign heads of state, however ghastly they may be, was recognizably the same as the 21-year-old Princess who spoke from South Africa to say, "I declare before you all that my whole life, whether it be long or short, shall be devoted to your service."

There are many moments during her long reign when even quite reasonably minded people have asked whether modern Britain had outlived the monarchy and its quasi-religious trappings, whether it would be more sensible to become like France or Germany or the U.S. and declare for a republic. In fact, the monarchy and the Monarch are arguably more popular now, after all these years, than at any other time in history.

Witness the huge crowds that came out to cheer during the Golden, Diamond, and Platinum Jubilees. And the awesome size of the crowds that came to witness her grandsons marry their respective brides.

LONG TO REIGN OVER US

Five years after she became Queen, a journalist named John Grigg—actually a very genial man who tried to become a Liberal member of Parliament—attacked the Queen in print for a string of offenses, among them, for having a voice that was "a pain in the neck" and for lacking spontaneity. She appeared to be just "going through the motions." He got slapped in the face for his temerity. The Queen went on reigning.

Long to reign over us, the British sang, when the nation began to emerge from the austerity years and Prime Minister Harold Macmillan told Britons they had never had it so good. Long to reign over us during the 1960s, when half the population had scarcely adequate plumbing or dentistry and homosexuality was still a criminal offense. Now there are openly gay cabinet ministers and bishops. Long to reign over us when the British governments of the 1970s recognized a changing public morality but bumblingly allowed the economy to fall into chaos, and when clashing ideologies led to a heated immigration debate throughout Britain. Elizabeth lived to see London become the financial powerhouse of Europe and to see Britain absorb a vast number of Asian and African immigrants with prodigious ease.

Wiseacres writing newspaper columns can supply any kind of reason that the monarchy should have grown in popularity. And undoubtedly, one of the reasons is that while the British all struggled to come to terms with the dazzling rate of change in British society, the head of state remained a constant.

But it would be very easy to imagine how the wrong hereditary figurehead during this period could have steered the institution of monarchy into the rocks. Look at what happened in Spain when King Juan Carlos slithered from being the white hope of a revived kingship to a paunchy playboy. Either he went or the monarchy went.

"I HAVE TO BE SEEN"

Elizabeth possessed a few ideal qualities for a modern monarch. One of these was her personal modesty. She appeared all over the place. Indeed, mindful of Queen Victoria's unwillingness to perform public duties, Elizabeth once said, "I have to be seen to be believed." Yet there was never a cult of personality, and she never wanted to be the center of attention. John Grigg was so wrong all those years ago: Going through the motions is the Monarch's job.

It is not true that she never let her political views become apparent. I have already cited her firm conviction that the Commonwealth was right to deplore the apartheid system in South Africa. Nearer home, she made no secret of the fact that she was crowned Queen of a United Kingdom and would like it to remain United. At the same time, when she went to Ireland, she gladdened the hearts not only of her Irish hosts but of onlookers all over the world by acknowledging the faults of both sides. It was not just her learning a bit of Irish to repeat at a state dinner; it was the silence and the head bowed as she remembered the Irish dead. Think how a British politician—any politician—would have been tempted to ham that up.

There is a legitimate debate to be had about whether Britain should still have an established church, and whether, for example, there should still be Church of England bishops in the House of Lords. What is not in question, however, is that the Queen as her own person was an unobtrusively devout woman whose Christian faith was central to her life. Because of this fact, that faith occupied center stage of national life on ceremonial occasions, such as the Armistice. While Britain became more secular and when public debate about religion became on occasion strident, Elizabeth showed in her own person that you can be a normal, quiet, decent person who still believes in God.

A Faithful Servant *Elizabeth with family at St. Paul's Cathedral participating in a thanksgiving service to mark her 50 years on the throne.*

A CAREER OF NOT BEING INTERESTING

There is almost no comparable figure of the world stage who has been prepared to do this. Even so gigantic a figure as Pope John Paul II could not help himself reinterpreting the role of the papacy, with his almost perpetual road show of appearances in sports stadiums around the world. Yes, he was flying the flag for the papacy and the Catholic religion, but—love him or loathe him—you were always aware of his overpowering personality. He did far more than go through the motions. The Queen did not do so. Her friends and the inner circle of race-goers, ladies-in-waiting, and so on can all share moments when the Queen has burst into laughter after the blundering behavior of some visiting dignitary, or emphasize her natural and enthusiastic cheerfulness when touring the stables at Balmoral or attending the races with chums such as Lord Porchester. But for the public, the strength of the Queen's personality was that she kept it hidden. She behaved as if she did not have one. She went through the motions. Most public figures dread being boring. Elizabeth's strength was the vigor with which she pursued a career of not being interesting.

To what extent this was a calculated decision, made all those years ago when she dedicated her life, long or short, to the service of the imperial family, we do not know. It was, however, a demeanor that made her so triumphantly successful as a constitutional monarch. British republicans can attack the institution of the monarchy, but they can only ever do so on a theoretical level. They cannot "descend to personalities," because, as far as the public is concerned, the Monarch did not have a "personality" in the sense that, say, her son Charles has. His celebrated letters to ministers of the Crown, setting out his views on every subject from unpasteurized cheese and genetically modified crops to the European Union and the People's Republic of China, would have been unthinkable coming from the pen of his mother. She did not go in for "views."

BEACON OF HOPE AND STABILITY

Silences, broken by a very few well-chosen words, marked her public style. She demonstrated that at Bergen-Belsen in 2015, when she and her husband, the late Prince Philip, visited the concentration camp as tottering old people, nearly all of whose ancestors had been German. There was no need for the kind of speech a politician would have made. The visit itself was a sort of healing of that family row that had begun in 1914 when Cousin George declared war on Cousin Willy and tens of millions of people got killed.

During a visit to Ireland in 2011, in a speech she began at a state banquet with a few Irish words, she called for "forbearance and conciliation." It was so unlike the preening or aggressive words the Irish people had been used to hearing from English politicians. She spoke for her people.

Chiefly, she spoke throughout her reign by her silences. Many of those who spoke with her—either intimates or those meeting her for a few moments—felt a sense of deep personal goodness. Such goodness can be a little frightening, for she embodies standards to which the rest of us cannot often measure up. I once asked Elizabeth's late sister, Princess Margaret, whether she was one of those many people who had dreams about the Queen. She was. She said it was always the same dream. That she had done something wrong of which the Queen furiously disapproved. One might suppose that this was simply a case of the Princess's dream life reflecting reality, but she said, "The Queen

is not in fact a censorious person, and she has never criticized me personally, in waking life. Only in my dreams. When I wake up after such a dream, I feel utterly wretched, as if I have been shut out of the love of God. I wake much later than she does, but when I have had such a dream, I always have to ring her up, even if it is midmorning and she is at work. I simply pick up the receiver, ring, and she says, 'Hello.' I say, 'Hello,' and ring off. All is well. I know that I still have her love."

The Queen was much more than a figurehead. She was an example of everything that was best about Britain: understated, good-hearted, horsey. She was also a beacon of hope and stability for the nation. When a suicide bomber attacked an Ariana Grande concert in Manchester in 2017, killing 22 people, many of them children, the Queen was there for her people. She visited the Royal Manchester Children's Hospital and comforted the recovering children and their parents. In that year's annual Christmas message, she addressed the attack: "I had the privilege of meeting some of the young survivors and their parents." The Queen continued, "I describe that hospital visit as a 'privilege' because the patients I met were an example to us all, showing extraordinary bravery and resilience."

Diamond Jubilee *Greeting crowds celebrating her 60 years as Queen during a visit to Leeds in 2012.*

Her Majesty's Homes

If you ever wondered where Elizabeth worked, celebrated, and rested, this is your guide.

BUCKINGHAM PALACE

The Royal Family's HQ

London, England

Buckingham Palace, home of the famous Changing of the Guard, has been the official residence of the U.K. sovereigns since 1837, but the history of the site dates back to King James I in the early 17th century. When you see a photo of the royal family waving from a balcony, it was likely taken at Buckingham Palace.

WINDSOR CASTLE

The Country Home

Windsor, Berkshire, England

Windsor Castle is the largest and oldest occupied castle in the world, founded in the 11th century. The Queen used it for both work and relaxation. Frogmore Cottage, a home belonging Prince Harry and Meghan, Duchess of Sussex, is also located on the property.

BALMORAL HOUSE

The Holiday House

Aberdeenshire, Scotland

Prince Albert purchased Balmoral House for Queen Victoria in 1852, and it was passed through the royal generations. It was a favorite holiday spot for the Queen—she particularly enjoyed riding horseback through the vast terrain on summer holidays.

THE PALACE OF HOLYROODHOUSE

The Scotland House

Edinburgh, Scotland

The Palace of Holyroodhouse is the official residence of the monarch in Scotland. The Queen stayed there for a week each year during what the Scottish call "Royal Week," where she held official engagements and visited Scottish regions.

SANDRINGHAM HOUSE

The Winter House

Sandringham, Norfolk, England

Purchased by the Royal Family in 1862, Sandringham House is a full-scale Victorian country home. Elizabeth spent about two months each winter there, arriving in time to celebrate Christmas and staying through February.

HILLSBOROUGH CASTLE

The Northern Ireland House

Royal Hillsborough, County Down, Northern Ireland

Hillsborough Castle is the official residence of the Secretary of State for Northern Ireland and for the royal family when they are in the area. Although the Queen conducted important business there in the past, she rarely visited in the later years of her life.

A Tried-and-True Ally

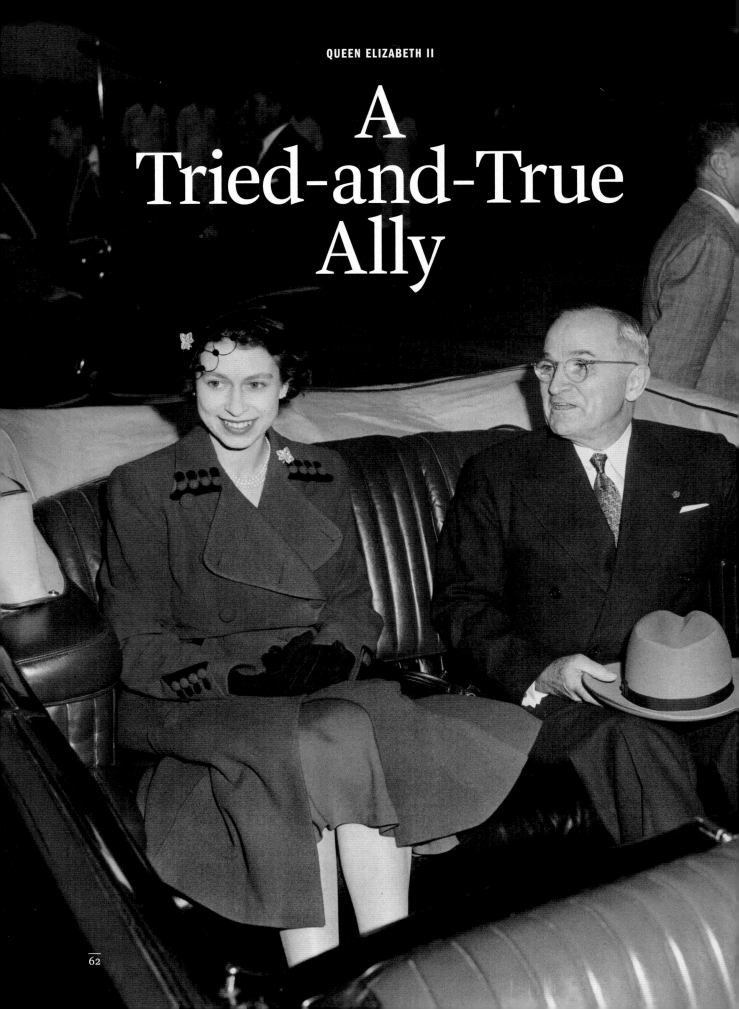

The First Trip *President Truman and Princess Elizabeth are shown in their motorcade following the reception ceremony at Washington National Airport on October 31, 1951.*

The Queen met 13 of the 14 U.S. presidents since Harry Truman took office in 1945— all except Lyndon B. Johnson. Here's what happened during the meetings.

BY CIARA NUGENT

HARRY TRUMAN

October 31, 1951, Washington, D.C.

Elizabeth was not yet a queen when, at the age of 25, she was first introduced to an American president. Harry Truman and his wife Bess hosted Elizabeth and Prince Philip on a two-day visit to Washington. Acting on behalf of her father, King George VI, who was gravely ill at the time, Elizabeth gave Truman an ornate 18th-century overmantel to hang above a fireplace in the White House. The president said that, while he had received many guests in Washington, "Never before have we had such a wonderful young couple, who have so completely captured the hearts of all of us."

DWIGHT D. EISENHOWER

October 17, 1957, Washington, D.C.

Elizabeth made her first state visit to the U.S. as Queen midway through Dwight D. Eisenhower's two terms as president. The visit came during the Cold War— a crucial time for the U.S.-U.K. alliance. British Prime Minister Harold Macmillan was also in town for talks with U.S. leadership. The Queen found time for more lighthearted events, including a state dinner, a visit to Jamestown, Virginia—site of the first British settlement in America—and her first American college football game.

Levity in Dark Times (above) *Elizabeth chats with President Eisenhower while Mamie Eisenhower laughs with Prince Philip at a White House state banquet in 1957.*

That Delightful Evening
At Buckingham Palace during a banquet held in his honor, President Kennedy and his wife, Jackie, pose with the Queen and Prince Philip.

JOHN F. KENNEDY

June 15, 1961, London

Half a million people turned out to greet the Kennedys when they arrived in London for a visit in 1961, just a few months after his inauguration. The Netflix series *The Crown* recreated the visit in its second season, making much of the first lady's alleged criticisms of the Queen's old-fashioned style. The royals hosted the Kennedys at a lavish dinner at Buckingham Palace, and the president later wrote to the Queen saying he would "always cherish the memory of that delightful evening."

RICHARD NIXON

February 15, 1969, London

Her Majesty had already met President Richard Nixon in 1957 when he was vice president under Dwight D. Eisenhower. But their first meeting as two heads of state took place in 1969, when Nixon made an informal visit to the United Kingdom shortly after taking office. The Queen and Prince Philip hosted Nixon at Buckingham Palace and exchanged signed photos of themselves, while a television crew captured the occasion for a documentary called *The Royal Family*, broadcast later that year.

The Grand Tour *Elizabeth with President Nixon, as they walk through the corridors of Buckingham Palace along with Prince Philip, Prince Charles, and Princess Anne.*

Four Stars *President Ford, dancing with Elizabeth at the ball at the White House during the 1976 U.S. bicentennial celebrations.*

GERALD FORD

July 17, 1976, Washington, D.C.

Shortly after the 200th anniversary of America's declaration of independence from Britain, the Queen came to Washington to celebrate the continuing relationship between the two countries with a state dinner hosted by Gerald Ford. The pair shared a dance, and the president promised Elizabeth, "The United States [has] never forgotten its British heritage." First Lady Betty Ford later wrote in her memoir that "the queen was easy to deal with" and "If I hadn't kept mixing up Your Highness and Your Majesty ... I'd give myself four stars for the way that visit went off."

JIMMY CARTER

May 7, 1977, London

A year after her visit for the American bicentennial, the Queen hosted Jimmy Carter at Buckingham Palace for a dinner with other heads of state during a NATO summit. Carter famously broke royal protocol by kissing the Queen Mother on the lips. She was apparently mortified, saying "Nobody has done that since my husband died."

A Break in Protocol *The Queen hosted President Carter and other heads of state in London for a NATO summit.*

A Cowboy at Home
Ronald Reagan enjoying a horseback ride with Elizabeth on the grounds of Windsor Castle.

No Lectures, Please
George H. W. Bush and Barbara Bush with the Queen and Prince Philip at Buckingham Palace.

RONALD REAGAN

June 7, 1982, Windsor

In 1982, traveling with his wife, Nancy, Ronald Reagan became the first American president to stay overnight at Windsor Castle. It was the first of three trips the Reagans made to see the Queen in the U.K., and she also visited their ranch near Santa Barbara, California, in 1983. Reagan wrote in his memoir that the 1982 trip was a "fairytale visit" and one of the most "fun" moments of his presidency. He said the highlight was horseback riding with Elizabeth while Nancy and Philip rode in a horse-drawn carriage. "I must admit, the queen is quite an accomplished horsewoman," he wrote.

GEORGE H. W. BUSH

June 1, 1989, London

George H. W. Bush was introduced to the Queen in 1989 in London. During the visit, Bush also met Prime Minister Margaret Thatcher, who, he wrote disparagingly in his memoir, gave him "a lecture on freedom." Elizabeth, meanwhile, took the Bushes on a tour of Buckingham Palace. The Queen reciprocated the visit with a trip to Washington two years later.

Making Peace *President Clinton and the Queen smile for the camera at the Guildhall prior to a celebratory banquet for the 50th anniversary of the D-Day invasion of Normandy.*

BILL CLINTON

June 4, 1994, Portsmouth

President Bill Clinton made several visits to the U.K. during his presidency, in part because of his involvement in the peace process in Northern Ireland. He first met Elizabeth at a banquet honoring the 50th anniversary of World War II's D-Day at Portsmouth Guildhall, in southern England. Six years later the Queen hosted Bill, Hillary, and Chelsea at Buckingham Palace for tea.

GEORGE W. BUSH

November 21, 2003, London

George W. Bush first met the Queen over lunch at Buckingham Palace during a six-day European tour in 2001, and in 2003 became the first U.S. president to make an official state visit to the U.K. It was the Queen's most controversial meeting with an American president—until Trump. To coincide with Bush's visit in November, around 100,000 people took to the streets to protest the Iraq War, reportedly costing the U.K. millions in security spending during the three-day visit. The demonstration culminated with protesters toppling an effigy of Bush, recalling scenes of the fall of Saddam Hussein's statue in Baghdad six months earlier.

A Tense Trip *George W. Bush walks with the Queen into the White Drawing Room at Buckingham Palace.*

BARACK OBAMA

May 24, 2011, London

Barack and Michelle Obama were introduced to Elizabeth and Philip on a state visit in 2011. The Obamas presented her with a set of memorabilia and photographs from her parents' trip to the U.S. in 1939. In return, she gave them a collection of letters exchanged between previous monarchs and U.S. presidents. Looking at the letters relating to the American Revolution, Obama joked, "That was only a temporary blip in the relationship." The Obamas met the Queen twice more, and on her 90th birthday the president said, "She is truly one of my favorite people."

Fast Friends *Barack Obama and the Queen during a state banquet at Buckingham Palace.*

DONALD TRUMP

July 13, 2018, Windsor

President Trump first met the Queen on an official visit in 2018, when they had tea at Windsor Castle. He largely avoided London, where tens of thousands of protesters turned out to criticize his rhetoric and policy on issues including migration, gender, and LGBTQ rights.

Up for Inspection *Elizabeth walks with President Trump as they inspect the Coldstream Guards at Windsor Castle.*

JOE BIDEN

June 13, 2021, Windsor

President Joe Biden and First Lady Jill Biden had tea with Her Majesty at Windsor Castle. Afterward, Biden told reporters that the Queen had been a gracious host. "I don't think she would be insulted, but she reminds me of my mother in terms of the look of her and just the generosity," he said. The Bidens left Elizabeth with an open invitation to visit them at the White House.

Warm Welcome *Queen Elizabeth and Joe Biden in the Grand Corridor at Windsor Castle.*

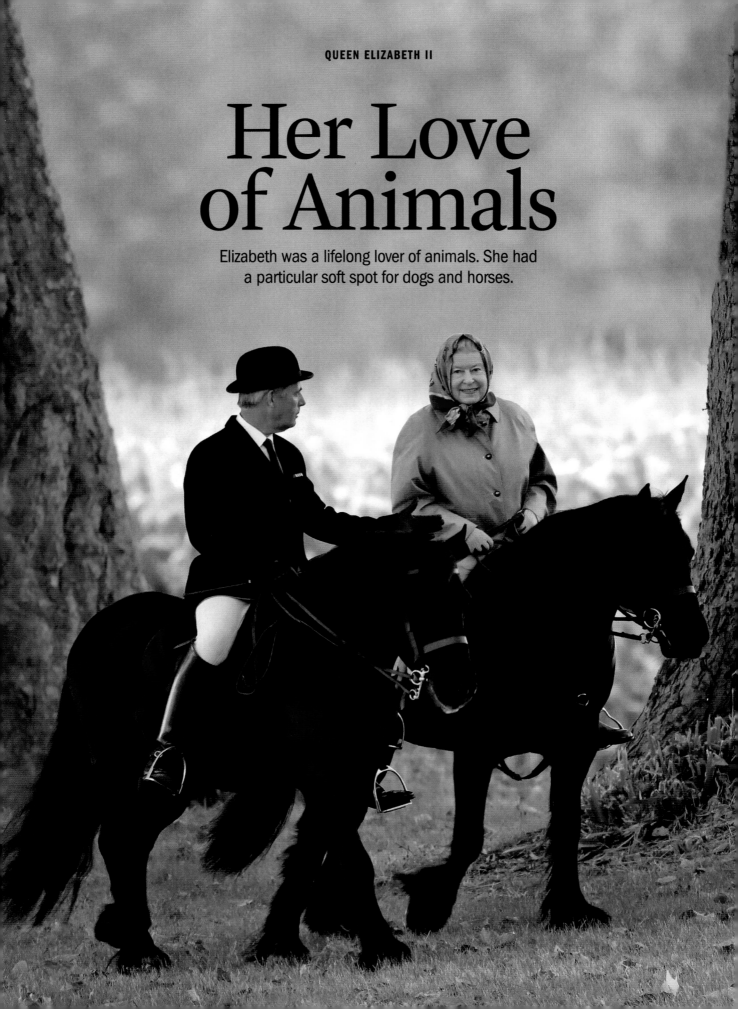

Her Love of Animals

Elizabeth was a lifelong lover of animals. She had a particular soft spot for dogs and horses.

Out for a Spin *(facing page) Elizabeth riding the grounds of Windsor Castle with her stud groom, Terry Pendry, in 2008.*

In the Garden *(left) The Queen poses with one of her corgis at Balmoral Castle in 1952.*

Happy Birthday *Young Elizabeth poses with her pony on her 13th birthday.*

Will Travel *The Queen arrives at Aberdeen Airport with her corgis in tow at the start of her annual holiday at Balmoral Castle in 1974.*

Fun Playmates *Ten-year-old Princess Elizabeth playing with her corgis at 145 Picadilly, London, in 1936. She is believed to have owned at least 30 corgis throughout her life.*

A Cultural Icon

Her Majesty's Hats A glimpse at the Queen's millinery through the years

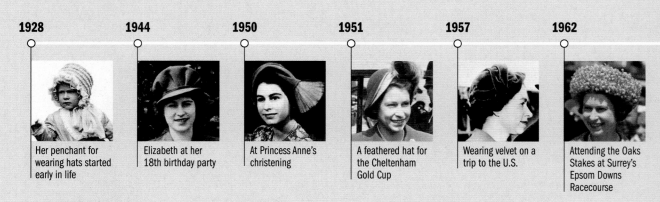

1928 — Her penchant for wearing hats started early in life

1944 — Elizabeth at her 18th birthday party

1950 — At Princess Anne's christening

1951 — A feathered hat for the Cheltenham Gold Cup

1957 — Wearing velvet on a trip to the U.S.

1962 — Attending the Oaks Stakes at Surrey's Epsom Downs Racecourse

The modern Elizabethan era spawned cultural movements, with literature and artifacts that are recognized to this day. What will be the cultural legacy of Queen Elizabeth II?

BY BELINDA LUSCOMBE

HER REGAL FACE

Queen Elizabeth II is very likely the most portrayed woman on the planet. Her head, by law, has been on every British stamp since she ascended the throne. Billions of stamps, millions of coins and notes, and hundreds of thousands of postcards bear her likeness. Her face is recognized in every English-speaking land and is ubiquitous in several. It is the face of distant historic authority, a literal figurehead, having no real power but oodles of symbolic supremacy.

Does ubiquity equal influence? The Queen did not inspire purchases the way other famous faces did. She could not give the sales of a certain brand of lipstick a jolt by casually dropping its name in conversation. But her complete lack of sex appeal or commercial appeal was actually the Queen's strength: It buttressed her rare and more potent qualities—consistency and longevity. Pop-culture figures come and go, but none were as durable as Her Majesty's regal face.

Symbolic Supremacy *(facing page) A woman admiring "Lightness of Being" by Chris Levine; (clockwise from top left) the pound coin designed in 2016; a solar-powered miniature figure of Elizabeth; stamps to celebrate her 90th birthday; a mug commemorating her Silver Jubilee; 90th birthday souvenir postcards.*

1965 On a royal visit to the Isle of Wight

1968 A floral selection for the Royal Society's Centenary Garden Party

1970 Pure '70s stye at the Epsom Derby

1975 A turban for the state visit to Mexico

1977 Pastel peach on a trip to New Zealand

1982 Wearing Frederick Fox on a tour of the South Pacific

THE PORTRAITS

Officially, Elizabeth sat for roughly 200 portraits by artists from Annie Leibovitz to Lucian Freud to hologram creator Chris Levine. She never gave her opinion on the results—at least not publicly—and seemed to regard lending her time to artists as part of her cultural duty. The painters didn't get to know their subject, because she could never be a subject. One artist—Justin Mortimer, whose portrayal stirred up controversy because it separated her head from her body—had two two-hour sittings with the Queen, mostly to take Polaroids and make sketches. "She sat very formally (like a queen) in her chair and was chatting nonstop to her equerry," he recalled afterward. "The second session was more relaxed but not intimate. We even talked. She was funny."

Of course, the Queen's official portraits, even those by masters such as Freud, are nowhere near as culturally relevant as her uncommissioned portrayals. She was vastly more influential as an icon than as a patron. As the apogee of all that is British and institutional and proper, Her Majesty served as a useful target. Unchanging and unknowable, she was a perfect canvas on which to project the obsessions of the moment. Andy Warhol's silkscreen prints of Elizabeth, part of his "Reigning Queens" series of the mid '80s, treated her like any other celebrity, frozen in time and bright colors. Even earlier, Jamie Reid gave her a baby pin through her nose, like a '70s punk. And in recent years she was rendered as a pinup by street artist Pegasus.

REBEL ART

It was Reid, too, who created the 1977 cover for the Sex Pistols single "God Save the Queen," which has become part of a robust body of work that defaced the Queen's image as a shorthand for rebellion or anti-establishment passion. The British TV show *Spitting Image* (1984-1996) used puppets to mock the royals, making them look dim or harried. In the late '90s, another show, *The Royle Family*, followed the escapades and interactions of a family that mirrored the Windsors in uncanny ways—right down to the fact that both clans lived off the government—except the Royles were broke.

More recently the mock-the-Queen approach has fallen out of vogue, with such artists as Alison Jackson examining instead the strangeness of the public appetite for intimate or embarrassing details about the royal family. Jackson gets lookalike actors to pose as, say, the Queen on the toilet reading a newspaper and photographs them in paparazzi style. The juxtaposition is uncomfortable, confronting readers with their own voyeurism: In a world full of artifice masquerading as reality, what images of the Western world's most gilded family do we seek out and create?

FASHION INFLUENCE

Perhaps the most interesting evolution of the Queen's cultural impact was seen in the fashion industry. Her clothing choices, never considered avant-garde or

Her Majesty's Hats

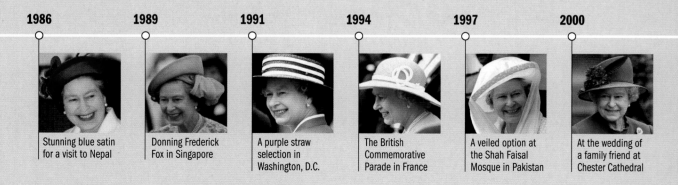

1986	1989	1991	1994	1997	2000
Stunning blue satin for a visit to Nepal	Donning Frederick Fox in Singapore	A purple straw selection in Washington, D.C.	The British Commemorative Parade in France	A veiled option at the Shah Faisal Mosque in Pakistan	At the wedding of a family friend at Chester Cathedral

even fashion forward, were most generously described as safe. Under the risible headline "Elizabethan look may capture Fashion World," the Pittsburgh *Press* of February 1952 praised the Queen's fashion choices and her "dainty waist and slim hips" but noted that Norman Hartnell, one of the couturiers to the Crown, said that "no member of the royal family intends to influence fashion." If that was her aim, it has been one of the Queen's most successful and lasting campaigns.

The point of Her Majesty's wardrobe was pretty much to wear what no one else would. She donned bright colors and bold prints so she could be easily spotted in a crowd. This tended to send the royal dresser to a lot of fuchsias, primrose yellows, and purples—and so much the better if those colors weren't fashionable.

Because she could not under any circumstances be considered underdressed, the Queen would often wear a matching hat, coat, and gloves. For a long time, this extreme matchiness was considered frumpy. But over the years, the Queen's highly coordinated, color-saturated look began to appeal to other women, particularly those in positions of prominence without power.

The trickle-down effect spilled over onto women who like to be contrary: British model Agyness Deyn cited the Sovereign as her fashion icon. "The Queen dresses all matching," noted *Vogue Japan* editor-at-large Anna Dello Russo. "What incredible impact that has. No one else dresses all in pink without looking hilarious, but she does. She pulls it off." Even the Queen's conspicuously dowdy casual wear, with its range of head scarves, wool skirts, and knee socks, was

aped: It was the inspiration for Dolce & Gabbana's fall 2008 ready-to-wear line.

All this must have been very reassuring to a monarch in her twilight years. She didn't have to change to keep up with the times. The times circled back to her.

Matchy-Matchy *Elizabeth wears fuchsia and a bold print to the 2008 Derby Festival at Epsom Downs.*

2005 The memorial service for tsunami victims at St. Paul's Cathedral

2009 At the unveiling of the Queen Elizabeth, The Queen Mother statue in London

2013 A visit to the Argyll & Sutherland Highlanders in Canterbury, England

2017 Attending the Royal Maundy service at Leicester Cathedral

2019 Her choice for the Commonwealth Day service at Westminster Abbey

2021 At the launch of the Queen's Baton Relay for Birmingham

The Crown Jewels

Discover the story behind some of the precious items used at Elizabeth's coronation ceremony in 1953.

THE DIAMOND DIADEM

This crown was originally made for King George IV's coronation. Elizabeth wore it on her journey to Westminster on her coronation day. It is made of gold and silver with pearls along the band, and it contains 1,333 diamonds, including a four-carat pale yellow brilliant in the center of the front cross. To the delight of the public, she wore it on other occasions including the opening of Parliament in 2006.

THE SOVEREIGN'S ORB AND SCEPTRE

The Sovereign's Orb, made in 1661, is a symbol of power and the Christian world, with a cross mounted on a globe. It is a hollow gold sphere girdled by a band of diamonds, emeralds, rubies, sapphires, and pearls with a large amethyst and cross at the top. It is placed in the hand of the monarch during the coronation ceremony.

The Sovereign's Sceptre with Cross has been used in every coronation since 1661. It is made of gold and precious gems, including rubies, diamonds, and emeralds. In 1910, the Cullinan I diamond was added for the coronation of King George V. The diamond is the largest top-quality cut white diamond in the world, weighing in at 530.2 carats (nearly 1/4 pound); in fact, the centurys-old sceptre had to be reinforced to handle the gem's weight. The significance of the sceptre presentation was described at the coronation of William the Conqueror in 1066: "by the sceptre uprising in the kingdom are controlled, and the rod gathers and confines those men who stray."

THE IMPERIAL STATE CROWN

The Monarch wears The Imperial State Crown to walk out of Westminster Abbey after coronation. It is also used for formal occasions. It contains some of the most historic jewels in the Queen's collection. The stone that is set in the center of the cross is known as "The Black Prince's Ruby" because it is said to have been given to Edward, Prince of Wales (known as the Black Prince) in 1367 by Pedro the Cruel, King of Castile. It is not actually a ruby—it's a semiprecious spinel. The Imperial State Crown contains 2,868 diamonds, 17 sapphires, 11 emeralds, 269 pearls, and 4 rubies. Elizabeth has worn the crown at several openings of Parliament. In a 2018 interview with the BBC, she described wearing it as "unwieldy." She said, "You can't look down to read the speech, you have to take the speech up" or it will fall off.

ST. EDWARD'S CROWN

St. Edward's Crown is only used at the moment of a monarch's crowning, so it is considered the most sacred of the Crown Jewels. It is set with tourmalines, white and yellow topaz, rubies, amethysts, sapphires, garnet, peridot, zircons, spinel, and aquamarines. It was made in 1661 for the coronation of Charles II to replace the medieval crown that was melted down in 1649. It is made of solid gold and platinum, so it is heavy, weighing almost 5 pounds. It is said that Elizabeth practiced wearing it before her coronation to get used to the weight.

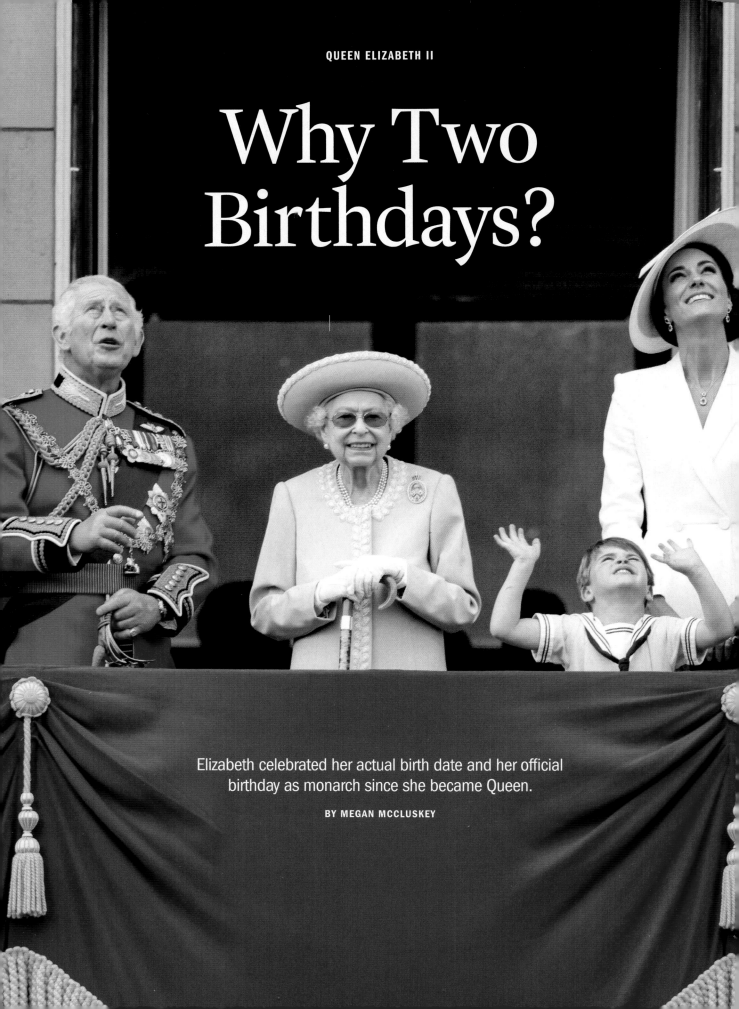

Why Two Birthdays?

Elizabeth celebrated her actual birth date and her official birthday as monarch since she became Queen.

BY MEGAN MCCLUSKEY

WHY DID THE QUEEN CELEBRATE TWO BIRTHDAYS?

Princess Elizabeth Alexandra Mary was born to the Duke and Duchess of York—later King George VI and Queen Elizabeth the Queen Mother—on April 21, 1926, making April 21 her real birthday. However, when she became Queen in 1952 following her father's death, she also began celebrating her official birthday.

Celebrating an official birthday as Monarch is a practice that started more than 250 years ago in 1748, when King George II decided that he wanted a better chance of good weather on his birthday than his November birth date afforded, according to the BBC. The King solved this problem by combining his birthday celebration with an annual military parade that took place each summer, beginning the double birthday tradition.

Since then, the second Saturday of June has become the usual date of any British monarch's official birthday.

HOW DID THE QUEEN CELEBRATE HER REAL BIRTHDAY?

Queen Elizabeth typically celebrated her real birthday with an intimate family gathering. But there were also three midday gun salutes—a 41-gun salute in Hyde Park, a 21-gun salute in Windsor Great Park, and a 62-gun salute at the Tower of London—to mark the occasion.

WHAT ABOUT THE QUEEN'S OFFICIAL BIRTHDAY?

Her Royal Majesty's official birthday was usually set on a Saturday in June and was celebrated with a big parade in London called Trooping the Colour. The impressive spectacle—which begins and ends at Buckingham Palace—featured hundreds of soldiers, horses, and musicians.

The Queen and several other members of the royal family participated in the processions before appearing on the Buckingham balcony as RAF planes performed aerial displays above the palace grounds.

In 2022, the Queen sat out of some of the Platinum Jubilee festivities, raising concerns about her health.

TIME

Queen Elizabeth II

Editor-in-Chief and CEO Edward Felsenthal
Executive Editor Ben Goldberger
Creative Director D.W. Pine
Design Director Chrissy Dunleavy
Director of Photography Katherine Pomerantz

Project Editor Julie Blume Benedict
Project Art Director Courtney Lentz
Project Copy Editor Catherine Cassidy
Editors Adam Rasmi, Karl Vick

President Ian Orefice
Chief Revenue Officer Viktoria Degtar
Partnerships Benjamin Katz, Michelle Evers
Retail Sales & Business Development Lisa MacDonald
Progress Marketing Maya Draisin

Credits

Cover
Richard Stone/Camera Press

Table of Contents
Terry Disney/Getty Images

2 Bettmann/Getty Images **3** WPA Pool/Getty Images **4** Popperfoto/Getty Images **5** Topical Press Agency/Getty Images **7** ullstein bild Dtl./Getty Images **8** Keystone-France/Getty Images **9** PA Images/Getty Images **11** Pool/Tim Graham Picture Library/Getty Images **12** Chris Jackson (3)/Getty Images; Comic Relief/Getty Images; David M. Benett (4)/Getty Images; David Rogers/Getty Images; Karwai Tang/Getty Images; Patrick Hertzog/Getty Images; Pool/Samir Hussein/Getty Images; Tom Wargacki/Getty Images; Visionhaus/Getty Images; WPA Pool (2)/Getty Images **13** Adam Davy/PA Images/Getty Images; Alan Crowhurst/Getty Images; Antony Jones/Getty Images; Chris Jackson (2)/Getty Images; Jean Catuffe/Getty Images; Joe Giddens/PA Images (2)/Getty Images; Matthew Horwood/Getty Images; Max Mumby/Indigo (4)/Getty Images **14** Bettmann/Getty Images **15** Chris Jackson (2)/Getty Images; Jean Catuffe/Getty Images; Karwai Tang/Getty Images; Max Mumby/Indigo (2)/Getty Images; **16** Alan Crowhurst/Getty Images; Antony Jones (2)/Getty Images; Chris Jackson (2)/Getty Images; David M. Benett/Getty Images; Visionhaus/Getty Images **17** Jeff Overs/Getty Images **18** Dominic Lipinski/Getty Images **19** Chris Jackson/Getty Images; Comic Relief/Getty Images; David Rogers/Getty Images; Joe Giddens/ PA Images/Getty Images; Max Mumby/Indigo (2)/Getty Images; Pool/Samir Hussein/Getty Images; WPA Pool/Getty Images **20** Max Mumby/Indigo/Getty Images **21** Dominic Lipinski/Getty Images **22** Chris Jackson/Getty Images **23** Transcendental Graphics/Getty Images; ullstein bild Dtl./Getty Images **24** Culture Club/Getty Images **25** Fox Photos (2)/Getty Images; Hulton Deutsch/Getty Images **26** Bettmann/Getty Images; Topical Press Agency/Getty Images **27** Hulton Archive (2)/Getty Images **28** Anwar Hussein/Getty Images; Hulton Deutsch/Getty Images **29** John Stillwell/Getty Images; Pool/Tim Graham Picture Library/Getty Images **30** AFP/Getty Images; Ben Stansall/Getty Images **31** Chris J Ratcliffe/Getty Images; Dominic Lipinski/Getty Images **32** Lisa Sheridan/Getty Images **34** AFP/Getty Images; Bettmann/Getty Images; Culture Club/Getty Images; Lisa Sheridan (2)/Getty Images; Mirrorpix (2)/Getty Images; Popperfoto/Getty Images; Universal History Archive/Getty Images **35** AFP/Getty Images; Bettmann/Getty Images; Hulton Archive/Getty Images; Hulton Deutsch/Getty Images; Lisa Sheridan/Getty Images; Mirrorpix/Getty Images; Stringer/Getty Images **36** Underwood Archives/Getty Images **37** Bettmann/Getty Images **38** Bryn Colton/Getty Images **39** Central Press/Getty Images **40** Keystone/Getty Images **41** Mirrorpix/Getty Images **42** Print Collector/Getty Images **44** Universal History Archive/Getty Images **47** AFP/Getty Images **48** Fiona Hanson/Getty Images **49** Fox Photos/Getty Images; Hulton Deutsch/Getty Images; Topical Press Agency/Getty Images; ullstein bild Dtl./Getty Images **50** Hulton Deutsch/Getty Images **51** AFP/Getty Images; Fox Photos/Getty Images **53** Topical Press Agency/Getty Images **55** Tim Graham/Getty Images **56** Anwar Hussein/Getty Images; Hulton Archive/Getty Images **57** Hulton Archive/Getty Images **58** Pool/Tim Graham Picture Library/Getty Images **59** WPA Pool/Getty Images **60** Chris Jackson/Getty Images; Heritage Images/Getty Images **61** AGF/Getty Images; Liam McBurney/PA Images/Getty Images; Radcliffe/Bauer-Griffin/Getty Images; Tim Graham/Getty Images **62** Bettmann/Getty Images **63** Keystone/Getty Images **64** John Olson/Getty Images; PhotoQuest/Getty Images **65** Henri Bureau/Getty Images; UniversalImagesGroup/Getty Images **66** Diana Walker/Getty Images; Tim Graham/Getty Images **67** Anwar Hussein/Getty Images; Tim Sloan/Getty Images **68** WPA Pool (2)/Getty Images **69** WPA Pool/Getty Images **70** Max Mumby/Indigo/Getty Images **71** Anwar Hussein/Getty Images; Bettmann/Getty Images; Central Press/Getty Images; Lisa Sheridan/Getty Images **72** AFP/Getty Images; Central Press/Getty Images; Fox Photos/Getty Images; Hulton Deutsch/Getty Images; Maeers/Getty Images; Print Collector/Getty Images; Tristan Fewings/Getty Images **73** Anwar Hussein (2)/Getty Images; Daniel Leal/Getty Images; Fox Photos/Getty Images; Gabriel Bouys/Getty Images; George Freston/Getty Images; Handout/Getty Images; Peter Dazeley/Getty Images; Science & Society Picture Library/Getty Images; Serge Lemoine/Getty Images; Tim Graham/Getty Images **74** Gareth Cattermole/Getty Images; Pool/Tim Graham Picture Library/Getty Images; Tim Graham (4)/Getty Images **75** Max Mumby/Indigo (6)/Getty Images; Tim Graham/Getty Images **76** Jonathan Brady/PA Images/Getty Images; Tim Graham/Getty Images **77** Hulton Deutsch/Getty Images; Stringer/Getty Images **78** Chris Jackson/Getty Images

Facing Page
Max Mumby/Indigo/Getty Images

Back Cover
Max Mumby/Indigo/Getty Images